# Permaculture Bible

An Ethical and Sustainable Approach to Living in Harmony with Nature, Using Organic Soil and Water to Grow and Design you Self-Sufficient Garden

**Krystle Barnett**

# Permaculture

## © Copyright 2023. All Rights Reserved.

The publication is sold with the idea that the publisher isnot required to render accounting, officially permitted orotherwise qualified services. This document is gearedtowards providing exact and reliable information concerning the topic and issue covered. If advice isnecessary, legal or professional, a practiced individual in the profession should be ordered.

- From a Declaration of Principles which was accepted andapproved equally by a Committee of the American Bar Association and a Committee of Publishers andAssociations.

In no way is it legal to reproduce, duplicate, or transmit anypart of this document in either electronic means or printedformat. Recording of this publication is strictly prohibited, and any storage of this document is not allowed unless with written permission from the publisher—all rights reserved.

The information provided herein is stated to be truthful andconsistent. Any liability, in terms of inattention orotherwise, by any usage or abuse of any policies, processes, or directions contained within is the sole and utterresponsibility of the recipient reader. Under nocircumstances will any legal responsibility or blame be held against the publisher for any reparation, damages, ormonetary loss due to the information herein, either directly or indirectly.

Respective authors own all copyrights not held by thepublisher.

The information herein is offered for informationalpurposes solely and is universal as so. The presentation of the information is without a contract or any guaranteeassurance.

The trademarks that are used are without any consent, andthe publication of the trademark is without permission or backing by the trademark owner. All trademarks andbrands within this book are for clarifying purposes only andare owned by the owners themselves, not affiliated with this document

# Table of Contents

**CHAPTER 1: INTRODUCTION TO PERMACULTURE**     7
    WHAT DOES PERMACULTURE MEAN,
    AND WHAT ARE ITS ADVANTAGES?     11
    HISTORY OF PERMACULTURE     15
    ETHICS AND DESIGN METHODOLOGIES OF PERMACULTURE     18
    AN OVERVIEW OF THE PRINCIPLES AND PRACTICES OF PERMACULTURE     22
    USING PERMACULTURE TO SHAPE THE FUTURE     26

**CHAPTER 2: PERMACULTURE IN THE GARDEN**     29
    TECHNIQUES FOR CREATING A PERMACULTURE GARDEN     33
    HOW TO INCREASE YOUR GARDEN'S PRODUCTION     36
    PERMACULTURE GARDENING IN URBAN AREAS     38

**CHAPTER 3: PERMACULTURE IN AGRICULTURE**     41
    STRATEGIES FOR CREATING A SUSTAINABLE
    AND RESILIENT AGRICULTURAL SYSTEM.     44
    PRODUCTION OF FOOD AND LANDSCAPING     45

**CHAPTER 4: WATER MANAGEMENT IN PERMACULTURE**     51
    TECHNIQUES FOR CAPTURING, STORING,
    AND USING WATER IN A PERMACULTURE SYSTEM.     54

**CHAPTER 5: ENERGY AND CLIMATE IN PERMACULTURE**     57
    STRATEGIES FOR REDUCING ENERGY CONSUMPTION AND MITIGATING
    THE IMPACTS OF CLIMATE CHANGE IN A PERMACULTURE SYSTEM.     60

**CHAPTER 6: PERMACULTURE IN THE COMMUNITY**     63
    STRATEGIES FOR CREATING PERMACULTURE COMMUNITIES     64

**CHAPTER 7: NATURAL BUILDING IN PERMACULTURE**     67
    TECHNIQUES FOR CREATING STRUCTURES
    THAT ARE IN HARMONY WITH THE ENVIRONMENT     70

**CHAPTER 8: PERMACULTURE EDUCATION AND OUTREACH**     81
    STRATEGIES FOR EDUCATING OTHERS ABOUT PERMACULTURE
    AND SPREADING ITS PRINCIPLES AND PRACTICES TO A WIDER AUDIENCE.     85

| | |
|---|---|
| **CHAPTER 9: PERMACULTURE FOR HEALTH AND WELLNESS** | **87** |
| **CHAPTER 10: PERMACULTURE PROJECTS** | **93** |
| **CHAPTER 11: FAQ** | **99** |
| **CONCLUSION** | **103** |
| **REFERENCES** | **104** |

# Chapter 1:

## Introduction to Permaculture

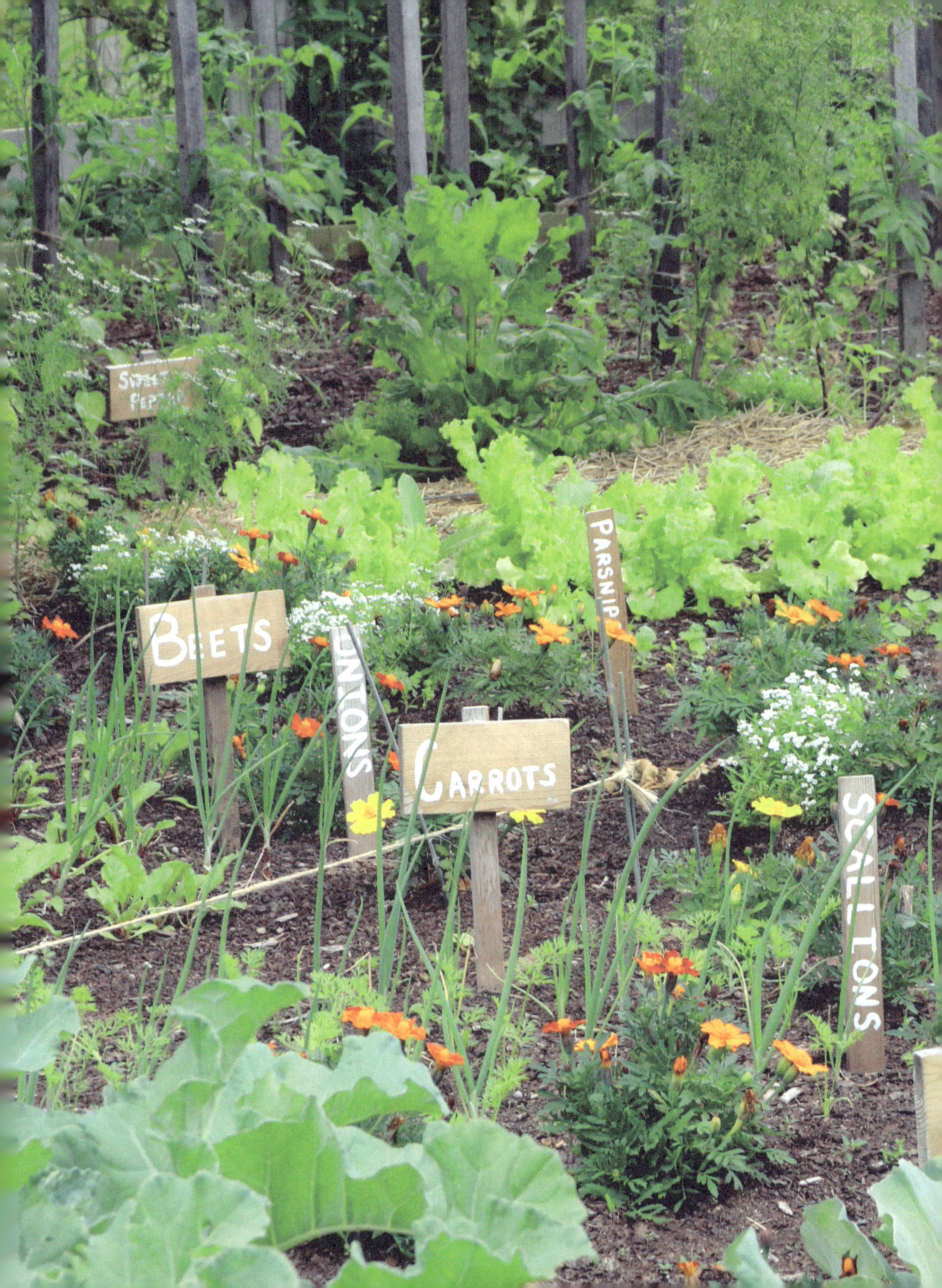
PARSNIP
BEETS
CARROTS
SCALLIONS

# CHAPTER 1: INTRODUCTION TO PERMACULTURE

The destructive effects of contemporary industrialized agriculture are everywhere. We observe lands stripped of their valuable topsoil, rivers, and other waterways contaminated by fertilizers and pesticides, and our woods felled to make room for crops.

In addition, our agricultural practices have significantly contributed to climate change. Our pursuit of efficiency has rendered us ineffective, and our pursuit of profit has rendered us wasteful.

It is possible to get considerably more out of life by consuming less by carefully considering how we use our resources, including food, energy, housing, and other material and non-material demands. With less work, we can produce more, benefiting both the environment and ourselves for the now and future. This is the cornerstone of permaculture principles and the key to creating a more sustainable future.

Permaculture is an ethical and principle-based design approach that can be used to develop, design, manage, and enhance all efforts made by people, families, and communities in the direction of a sustainable future.

Permaculture is a design philosophy and set of techniques for creating sustainable human settlements and agricultural systems. It is based on observing and mimicking natural ecosystems, using efficient energy and resource management, and creating mutually beneficial relationships between system components.

Permaculture can be applied to many areas, including farming, gardening, architecture, and community development.

Australians Bill Mollison and David Holmgren created it for the first time in the 1970s. The concepts of permanent agriculture and permanent culture were used to create the term permaculture, and it is now used to refer to agriculture that is always sustainable. We are encouraged to be resourceful and independent by Permaculture.

One of the best things about Permaculture is that it can be applied to any type of human environment, including urban apartments and window boxes, suburban and country homes, allotments, community spaces, farms and estates, business and industrial sites, educational institutions, and even unused land.

Every component of a permaculture system is designed by practitioners using their understanding of ecological systems and theory, ensuring that each component is advantageous to the system and that the relationships between components work to support the system. We ensure that the land may be used indefinitely by building strong, supportive connections that enhance the condition of the land while also maximizing its productivity.

Making waste from any of the humans, animals, plants, or activities in the permaculture system valuable to another element of the system—much like nature recycles everything—is one approach to do this. This ensures that nutrients stay in the body and eliminate the need to add more, reducing the amount of money and effort used and the pollution of water resources.

The idea of diversity is a crucial factor for permaculture practitioners. Contrary to modern agriculture, which frequently produces large quantities of a single crop, Permaculture depends on a vast array of various plants and animals.

In addition to the fact that the pest does not affect many other species, if a pest attacks one species, there is a significant possibility that something else in the system will go after the pest. If a pest attacks contemporary agriculture, the entire crop is lost.

No matter if you're managing a window box or a rainforest, permaculture design and practice are based on ethics that always apply. these guiding principles are;

Recognizing that earth is the source of all life and may even be a living being herself, that earth is a precious home, and that we are a part of the earth, not separate from it, is what is meant by **"earth care."**

People encourage and aid one another in changing methods of living that do not hurt us or the environment and in creating healthy societies because they care.

**Fair share** (or limiting consumption) ensures that the planet's finite resources are utilized wisely and equitably.

### WHAT DOES PERMACULTURE MEAN, AND WHAT ARE ITS ADVANTAGES?

Most people have certainly heard the phrase "**permaculture**" at some point. Still, unless we're already interested in the subject, we might not fully understand what it is, what it comprises, or even how it relates to sustainability. Even gardeners already utilizing some concepts and tenets might not know how Permaculture relates to what they do!

The term "**permaculture**" was first used in the 1970s by David Holmgren, then a student of Australian Bill Mollison. It is made out of the phrases agriculture and permanent.

Designing human homes and agricultural systems resembling nature is called Permaculture. Each element and its interactions with other aspects are considered while designing a permaculture system. Always taken into consideration are factors such as soil, living structures, plants, animals, microclimates, weather, and more.

Permaculture is a system of production that relies on sustainable resources and a self-sustaining ecosystem to support perpetual agriculture or horticulture.

In other words, it's a strategy for developing agricultural systems that support the land's natural environment and human settlement systems. This implies that you are creating sustainable land use plans using ecological and biological principles, which frequently mimic nature and produce the greatest possible output with the least effort. The only ethical decision is to assume responsibility for our existence and offspring.

The goal of Permaculture is to create ecological harmony within the system. A perfectly balanced system uses all of its resources, does not require external changes, and allows one product to feed another. For instance, a basic permaculture farm would feed its crops—which in turn would feed the animals—with animal excrement. Just enough crops and animal products (such as meat, eggs, etc.) are produced simultaneously to feed the human population. A system this simple has the potential to develop over time into a very complex ecosystem all on its own.

Contrary to traditional farming practices, Permaculture is a form of agriculture. Compared to conventional agriculture, it is more likely to be complicated, environmentally conscious, and long-term focused. It entails crop diversification, co-growing several crops in the same space, and utilizing more perennial plants.

Many of the principles utilized in this style of farming are extremely old and traditional and can be found in many indigenous cultures worldwide. Although the phrase permaculture is relatively new, it initially appeared in the term permanent agriculture, which was coined in 1929.

Looking at typical Western agriculture and making the things we take for granted conscious helps to understand Permaculture and how it differs from normal agriculture.

## WESTERN AGRICULTURE TODAY

Crop monocultures are a hallmark of contemporary Western agriculture. Usually, the land is cleared and divided into plots to cultivate various crops. The crops are typically boxed out in some way, either in terms of time or area. They may be cycled yearly or divided into patches or strips. Many crops raised in this manner are annuals only cultivated for a single season. In Western agriculture, cultivated or farmed land frequently spans for kilometers, with just minimal natural areas acting as buffers.

All of these presumptions or conventions are broken by Permaculture. Growing different crops on the same plot is common in Permaculture since it boosts overall productivity and minimizes pest and weed issues.

Concern over sustainable food production led to the development of modern Permaculture. It all began with the idea that people should not rely on industrialized agriculture, which uses fossil fuel-powered machinery, if they want to live sustainably. Low-input farming practices and a variety of crops are valued in Permaculture. The profusion of small-scale markets and home gardens for food production is a fantastic example.

## PERMACULTURE IS BASED ON ECOLOGICAL PRINCIPLES.

The distinction between mechanical and ecological agricultural methods can be regarded as the contrast between Permaculture and traditional Western agriculture. Permaculture is built on collaborating with nature, unlike Western agriculture, which aims to tame or dominate nature.

As a result, Permaculture necessitates a deeper comprehension of plants, animals, and their interrelationships, yet it has the potential to be extremely beneficial.

Permaculture uses tried-and-true technologies for food, energy, shelter, and infrastructure to build dependable, productive systems that meet human needs while integrating the land and those who occupy it. This would involve incorporating into the design the ecological processes of plants and animals, their nutrient cycles, climate conditions, weather cycles, and their interdependence.

A permaculture system uses concepts that may be used everywhere, on any scale, from one individual home to large regions, to minimize effort, turn "waste" into a resource, boost productivity and yields, and restore habitats.

## PERMACULTURE'S PROS AND BENEFITS

When you hear the word "permaculture," you might not know exactly what it means. However, dissecting the term clarifies that it refers to planning and constructing natural areas and food supply. Permacultures can be divided into two parts: agriculture that sustains communities and permanent, sustainable cultures.

To establish sustainable settings, Permaculture involves planting natural crops on land that is kept free of chemicals and machinery, allowing animals to graze there organically, and recycling natural resources back into the ground. Or, to put it another way, living as our forefathers did, and old things get a new lease on life.

In addition, Permaculture promotes energy-efficient construction, recycling, co-villages, housing, and social structures mimicking the village that once served as the community's source of sustenance. Imagine doing it in a city. The locals raise their food, which helps to keep the community alive. Everyone should cultivate, consume organic food and products, live in a caring atmosphere, and contribute financially to the community. Money generated locally is also spent locally.

Increased crop productivity is among Permaculture's most obvious and convincing advantages. In Permaculture, which combines numerous crops on the same plot of land, the total production of all combined crops can be substantially higher, even though Western monoculture farming is frequently the way to get the maximum yield per acre of a single crop. This can result in greater overall food output for homeowners and greater income for commercial growers.

Additionally, Permaculture lessens the demand for inputs like fertilizer and frequently removes the requirement for pesticides and herbicides altogether.

Diversified permaculture techniques may require more labor during the initial setup, but they can considerably reduce the need for long-term maintenance, notably weeding.

Permaculture also lessens pollution by recycling chemical inputs and organic waste products from plants and animals, using them as fertilizer. The outcome is a huge win for both sustainability and productivity.

## TENACITY AND FLEXIBILITY

In the face of exceptionally dry, wet, hot, or cold spells or other weather anomalies, Permaculture is also considerably more robust. Since different plants have varying degrees of resilience to various unfavorable environments, the greater diversity of crops offers one buffer or security mechanism.

However, the higher total biomass also correlates to increased resilience of the farming system to adverse weather events since it corresponds to more water stored, a stronger wind buffer, and a greater cooling capability in hot weather.

Crop diversity serves as a financial cushion to shield farmers against price swings, such as a crop glut that could result in lower prices for that specific year.

As a result, the system becomes more durable, stable, and predictable over time, in addition to being more productive.

## EXAMPLES OF CONVENTIONAL PERMACULTURE

The three sisters, beans, corn, and squash, are a strategy of growing three plants together that Native Americans commonly employ in North America. These crops complemented one another in both an ecological and dietary sense. The upright corn would serve as a pole up which the beans could climb.

Although the beans were a nitrogen fixer, the corn had significant nitrogen requirements. The sprawling squash, which also had a vining tendency, would cover the ground and keep weeds out. The squash also keeps moisture in the ground by covering it. Compared to beans or maize alone, the crop harvest creates a complete protein for the human diet.

The VAC system, which stands for "orchard," "fish pond," and "shed" for chickens or pigs in Northern Vietnam, is another traditional permaculture system from a distinct culture and ecoregion. This extremely productive system generates fiber, fuel, and meals for plants and animals. Animal waste is used as fertilizer, while fish are caught for output and pigs' food. With this approach, farmers can earn 3–5 times as much money as they would from growing rice alone while significantly lowering pollution.

Compared to Western agriculture, Permaculture is more complex, requires more knowledge and training, and frequently requires a larger initial labor investment. However, the benefits can be enormously compelling, including high overall crop yields, increased farmer income, greater stability, and significantly reduced environmental impacts.

## HISTORY OF PERMACULTURE

Permaculture was developed in the 1970s by Australian ecologists Bill Mollison and David Holmgren. They coined the term "permaculture" to describe a holistic method of designing sustainable human settlements and agricultural systems.

Bill Mollison witnessed the Industrial Revolution's growth as a monster and its effects on our culture.

How this kind of culture, with its insatiable thirst, was destined to succumb at some point. He decided to respond to this in a way that was more constructive than negative.

He discovered various things about how nature passes through sustainable cycles without the aid of humans by researching nature. Bill started by practicing and then teaching his ideas.

Masanobu Fukuoka is another figure who has subtly gained support within this movement. He thinks that the earth should be disturbed as little as possible. The soil is seeded directly on the surface, and the seeds are then lightly mulched with straw or another fine material.

Before they bloom, weeds are cut and allowed to mix with the mulch. This eliminates undesirable plants without poison and provides good soil for planting. Weeds and pests are less of an issue as the soil improves over time.

Another voice in this community is Ruth Stout. Many people's perspectives on weeds and weeding have changed due to her "no-till" gardening concepts. She claimed, like Fukuoka, to never require weeding and to permit plants to flourish nearby.

The soil is built by all plants, both "good" and "bad," and healthier crops produce fewer bugs. Weeding becomes as simple as flicking the weed out once the soil has been constructed without pesticides or herbicides.

Helen and Scott Nearing were pioneers of the US's sustainable and well-balanced "permaculture" lifestyle. According to Australian pioneers Bill Mollison and David Holmgren, the three guiding principles of permaculture are taking good care of the land, taking good care of people, and sharing what you have with others. In the 1970s, these men established the foundational ideas of permaculture.

Amid the Great Depression, in 1932, the Nearings family started their permaculture journey. At that time, they relocated to a farm in Vermont and started farming their food.

They made an effort to divide their days into blocks of time that encouraged the care of the land and food production, followed by blocks that encouraged personal development since they also believed in establishing a balance between work and leisure. Many people did not just follow the Nearings' lead; some did so literally.

Many young people started a "back to the earth" movement in the late 1960s when the "counter-culture" movement was raging in the United States to forge a stronger bond with the environment they intuitively knew supported them.

Eliot Coleman and his wife Sue were among those who followed Helen and Scott Nearing. They bought 60 acres of land from the Nearings in 1968 after being inspired by the 1954 book Living the Good Life, and they taught themselves how to grow food organically. They intended to lead a sustainable lifestyle free of all contemporary luxuries. In the 1980s and 1990s, Coleman became a leader in the US in better food, organic fertilizer, and lifestyle movements. The New Organic Grower, published in 1989, was written by him.

Some find it intriguing that the Nearings' 1930s lifestyle, which was adopted by many others, promoted permaculture ideas long before the term was even coined. But when you think about it, this movement might be the most conservative. It merely represents a return to a previous era's way of life. To live a decent life today, one must strive to use nature without destroying it, which does not always involve giving up many or even most of the contemporary amenities.

To recycle and reuse as much as possible, generate as much of one's power as feasible, consume complete foods that one has prepared themselves, and assist others in achieving similar objectives.

The Nearings were probably among the first to seek to live such a life in the modern, post-industrial world, albeit they were by no means the first to do so. The first settlers to this "new world" had to manufacture, cultivate, or build everything they needed.

Permaculture will need to be adopted to some extent from its humble, revolutionary beginnings. Industrial waste pollution and mass transit system pollution are relics of the past. Food grown locally or produced by the consumer makes more and more financial sense because importing food from other parts of the country will be too expensive.

One might argue that Permaculture is a philosophy of using the land based on the natural energy patterns and material flows from inside nature if asked to characterize it as a system. It is one of the world's most comprehensive systems for analysis and design.

Permaculture is a "land use planning" ideology, not just a specific production technique. Its principles can be applied globally to farms, houses, local communities, and cities. It is site-specific and, therefore, adaptive to regional microclimates, cultures, and production methods.

Sir Albert Howard, the founder of the organic farming movement, was renowned for providing practical answers to farming issues. He emphasized promoting the composting of plant wastes and human and animal manure to improve the soil. This can be used safely to restore soil fertility, as we know. Additionally, it is more sensible than purchasing pricey chemical fertilizers.

Permaculture prioritizes design over knowledge of a plant's characteristics and nutritional needs. While it is true that Permaculture favors perennial plants over annual ones in many situations, annuals nevertheless have a place in Permaculture systems. Gardens would suffer if they did not contain beans, salad crops, parsley, basil, and radishes.

Tomatoes, peas, and beans are annual plants in home vegetable gardens, and the garden needs legumes to help deliver nitrogen. Perennials, biennials, and annuals work well together to make a successful organic garden.

Although most people would agree that achieving complete self-sufficiency in a typical backyard is unachievable, we should all strive to be self-sufficient in some areas. It's not difficult for every country to produce enough food, and Australia and other nations might be able to produce their seeds, fruits, and vegetables. Even the popular herbal remedies sold at health food stores contain fewer than 5% locally grown and processed components.

People worldwide are interested in learning how to develop societies and lead healthy, regenerative lifestyles compatible with all of earth's biological systems.

Adopting diets that support human health and the planet's ability to support our children, grandchildren, and future generations is one of the most crucial aspects of integrating with the environment.

Organic gardening is just a strategy of working with nature rather than against it, recycling natural resources to preserve soil fertility, and supporting natural ways of pest and disease control rather than depending on chemicals to do the job. It is not mystical or magical in any way.

## ETHICS AND DESIGN METHODOLOGIES OF PERMACULTURE

As more individuals become aware of its advantages, Permaculture's fundamental ethics are progressively gaining popularity. It was often believed that only third-generation hippies were interested in it.

Still, nowadays, it is commonplace in cities where people maintain their vegetable gardens and use the trimmings and unwanted bits as mulch. It is encouraging to see that something intrinsically beneficial to society on a global scale positively influences everyone in our lives.

Researching, observing, and comprehending the land's natural elements before converting it into a farm is crucial for permaculture design planning. Along with all of the natural resources present, it is important to consider the natural and artificial boundaries that define this system.

Thanks to these parameters, the permaculture system, application, and design are then steadily maintained over time. This design technique is incredibly original and imaginative, and actually, this is what makes the system work so well.

These designs include key ideas from natural patterns (like a spiral or wave shape). More patterns aim to cut waste.

Permaculture usually employs layers to produce an effective use of space. As a result, the use of space is maximized, and a supportive ecology can develop.

Permaculture uses natural processes to design ecologically sound agriculture systems. A permaculture system should enable a far higher degree of independence from human input for system care once it has been built. From a modest residential block to a huge farm, Permaculture may be adapted to fit any available land for the project.

Concern for the environment, people, and future are all Permaculture's elements. The goal is continuous environmental improvement. It considers the people's physical and mental welfare regarding the provision of food and shelter and the decrease in the labor necessary to maintain the system.

It reflects our concern for resource conservation, accomplished by recycling, renewable resources, and suitable planning that allows diverse system components to cooperate.

Dividing the garden space into several zones is a crucial component of the practical implementation of a permaculture garden. This entails setting up the garden's several zones concerning one another properly. It is easy to use time and energy more efficiently by placing the zones that need the greatest attention closer to the house.

Understanding natural processes and utilizing them for the harmonious growth of the garden are prerequisites for practicing Permaculture. When the system functions as it should, you will profit from nature participating in your dream rather than against it. You'll come to understand that collaborating with nature is considerably more fruitful than competing with it.

The deliberate design and maintenance of agriculturally productive ecosystems that have natural ecosystem diversity, stability, and resilience is known as permaculture. It is the harmonious coexistence of people and the environment, meeting their sustainable needs for food, energy, housing, and other material and non-material demands. A stable social order is impossible without constant agriculture.

Permaculture design combines conceptual, practical, and strategic elements that benefit life in all forms."

Adopting the permaculture design philosophy allows you to design systems based on nature's cycles. Instead of concentrating on individual components, you want to maximize beneficial connections between them and the final design's synergy.

No waste, no irrigation, and high-yielding land utilization with minimum effort are all hallmarks of permaculture. Permaculture farms produce as much as their contemporary equivalents, but the system relies less on hefty gear and more on letting nature take its course.

## PERMACULTURE IS BASED ON 12 DESIGN CONCEPTS.

1. Watch and engage.
2. Obtain and conserve energy.
3. Acquire a yield.
4. Use self-control and be open to criticism.
5. Utilize and value services and resources that are renewable.
6. Make no waste.
7. from patterns to details, design
8. Instead of segregating, integrate.
9. Make moderate, modest changes.
10. Utilize and treasure diversity.
11. Utilize the margin and value the edges.
12. Utilize change and react to it creatively.

The permaculture philosophy strongly emphasizes taking care of the system's participants, and this care encompasses the self-care you should practice and the community-focused care you should exhibit. After all, it should not be overlooked that arguably our biggest resource is yourself if you are concerned with healthy and sustainable connections within the various components of Permaculture.

According to Permaculture, we should reduce our resource usage to live sustainably. We are better off using the manure produced by animals already a part of our permaculture system than if we have to travel somewhere to acquire it, using fuel. Instead of mowing with a mower or cutting with a slasher pushed by a tractor, grass that has to be kept in check should be used as animal feed. So this method develops a resource in the form of manure that can be utilized to improve fertility and structure in the garden, as opposed to having to use resources like fuel in an unsustainable way. These are straightforward but effective illustrations of sustainable living.

The chicken is a perfect example of a valuable animal in a permaculture garden. Chickens pick up any dropped fruit or garden waste, make rich garden beds, and scrape around straw and hay to make great mulch. And at the end, they will give you eggs as payment.

**Permaculture's design methodologies are based on three core ethics:
Earth Care, People Care, and Fair Share.**

**EARTH CARE:** Care of the Earth is the opposite of most of what is now taking place on the land in most of the world; it involves cooperating with nature instead of doing so.

This ethic emphasizes the importance of protecting and regenerating natural ecosystems and reducing the human impact on the environment.

Keep the earth healthy by ensuring all living systems can endure and grow since humans cannot thrive without a healthy world.

**PEOPLE CARE:** This ethic encourages the design of systems that meet the needs of all people, including future generations. It also emphasizes the importance of community-based decision-making and empowering people to take control of their lives.

No matter where you reside, you can embrace an environmentally sound lifestyle for yourself or entire communities.

Provide access to the resources people need to survive by taking care of their needs.

**FAIR SHARE:** This ethic encourages the design of systems that share resources and benefits equitably and minimize waste and unnecessary consumption.

It also involves Limiting Population and Consumption in acknowledgment of the earth's finite resources and the fact that many billion people need a fair share of those resources around the world.

In healthy natural systems, surpluses from one element feed other parts of the system. And so may we, as humans. By controlling our own needs, we may borrow money to support the values above.

Permaculture design methods are based on observation and pattern recognition and focus on creating mutually beneficial relationships between the different elements in the system. The design process involves observing the site, identifying the key elements and resources, and organizing them to maximize their productive relationships.

Permaculture has been adopted worldwide, mainly in rural and suburban areas and urban settings. Permaculture design can be applied to small-scale and large-scale systems, from a home garden to a city neighborhood, from a small farm to a regional landscape.

Permaculture has grown to include many branches, such as regenerative agriculture, agroforestry, green architecture, and urban planning. It continues to evolve as a way to design a resilient and regenerative future for humanity and the planet.

## A PERMACULTURE DESIGN SYSTEM'S MAIN COMPONENTS ARE AS FOLLOWS:

**WATER** - The most significant component of Permaculture may be water gathering. Life is based on water. Both plants and animals require water to survive, which is necessary for washing, cooking, and cleaning. An important component of a permaculturalist's backyard is a rainwater tank, and it's also essential to collect grey water for use in the garden. Swales are used on larger properties to gather, redirect, or slow water flows down banks and slopes.

**ANIMALS** - On backyards and small properties, chickens offer a consistent supply of eggs and meat. Rabbits are also widespread and offer both meat and fur. Young rabbits can be ready to eat by 8 to 12 weeks of age if the correct breed is chosen. Cattle, goats, sheep, and pigs supply meat, milk, and leather on bigger properties.

**POWER GENERATION** - Permaculture systems can use various power sources, including solar panels, generators, and backyard wind turbines. Even though many permaculturalists want to be as self-sufficient as possible, most Suburban Permies continue to utilize mains electricity.

**HOUSING:** I have witnessed numerous homes constructed with permaculture ideas, from dwellings coated in mud to homes made of straw bales and built with mud bricks created on the property. There is the usage of conventional building supplies and techniques.

**FRUIT, VEGETABLES, AND GRAINS** – A list of organically grown fruits, vegetables, and grains would be incomplete. You and the animals must consume food, and compost is built on top of plants. Numerous veggies and salad greens can be cultivated all year long in various locations.

The few elements stated above are only a small portion of what Permaculture is. To feed the world one backyard at a time, Permaculture has a solid foundation. It necessitates assuming personal responsibility and offers a level of autonomy unmatched by any external governing system.

## AN OVERVIEW OF THE PRINCIPLES AND PRACTICES OF PERMACULTURE

Permaculture is just a system of design. One that is founded on moral principles and uses conventional, tried-and-true methods, acceptable technologies, and best practices. It cooperates with nature by adhering to its rules and functions.

The most fundamental ethical values are to protect the environment, take good care of humans (and all other living things), and ensure that everyone receives a fair share of all profits.

Permaculture has been described as a "toolbox" including elements from other disciplines.

Permaculture addresses the various layers that support and accommodate human life, including, at the most fundamental level, the acquisition of water, the production of food and shelter, the management of animal systems, the generation of energy, and the processing of "wastes" to be reinvested into the system as resources.

We can learn from permaculturists how to build natural structures, grow food, repair ecosystems and landscapes, collect rainwater, and do much more. Being a broad-based and holistic approach, Permaculture has numerous applications to all facets of life. The heart of permaculturists should be based on "values" or ethics that will hold regardless of the circumstance.

## PERSONAL AND PROFESSIONAL ATTRIBUTES OF PERMACULTURISTS

The earth is the source of life, our priceless home, and we are a part of it, not separate from it. A permaculturist should have Earthcare. To transform our way of living to one that is not destructive to the earth or ourselves, people should also care about, support, and assist one another. Finally, those who want to practice Permaculture should always think about their fair share and ensure that the planet's finite resources are used wisely and equally. This defines Permaculture as a green profession.

You'll save time and money by implementing permaculture principles in your garden and yard. Allow nature to work for you, then get the rewards.

Permaculture is based on several core principles, including:

**OBSERVE AND INTERACT:** This principle encourages the observer to examine the natural systems they are working with closely and to take time to understand the relationships and interactions between different elements.

**CATCH AND STORE ENERGY:** This principle involves capturing resources when they are abundant and storing them for times when they are scarce. This can include capturing rainwater, using solar energy, or preserving food.

**OBTAIN A YIELD:** This principle emphasizes the importance of producing food, fiber, and other resources from the land.

**APPLY SELF-REGULATION AND ACCEPT FEEDBACK:** This principle encourages using methods that minimize the need for external inputs and maintenance, paying attention to the feedback from the system, and making adjustments as needed.

**USE AND VALUE RENEWABLE RESOURCES:** This principle encourages using renewable resources, such as solar energy and compost, and recognizes the value of ecosystem services, such as pollination and soil formation.

**PRODUCE NO WASTE:** This principle emphasizes the importance of using all resources efficiently and finding a productive use for waste products.

**DESIGN FROM PATTERNS:** This principle encourages the observer to study natural systems patterns and use these patterns as a guide in designing human systems.

In addition to these principles, Permaculture also includes a variety of specific practices, such as:

**COMPANION PLANTING:** It involves planting different crops together to benefit both plants.

**MULCHING:** It involves covering the soil with organic material to retain moisture and suppress weeds.

**SWALES:** These shallow trenches are used to slow and store water on a landscape.

**POLYCULTURES:** This is the practice of growing multiple crops in the same area to increase productivity and create mutually beneficial relationships between plants.

Permaculture is not only gardening but also an approach to thinking, design, and problem-solving that can be applied to all areas of human life, from agriculture to architecture, community development, and economic systems.

It is consequently possible to adapt all of these support systems—including those for water, energy, waste management, food production, and animal systems—to the principles and designs of Permaculture.

**WATER.**

All life depends on water. We are, after all, roughly 60% water.

While obtaining water is a significant aspect of daily living in many parts of the world, few people typically consider the source of their water in affluent nations. Water is available when we open the faucet, and customers of municipalities receive water from them, so how could anyone ever consider that there might be alternatives?

Climate, precipitation, seasons, and rain cycle are all unique to each place on earth.

With careful planning, it is reasonable to say that a lot of water may be gathered from the sky as it falls on a site. This is especially true if a building with a roof can collect and guide the water to appropriate storage systems (in tanks or the soil). In areas with low annual precipitation averages, doing so is feasible and crucial.

It is possible to gain a variety of advantages by using this technique.

High-quality water reserves can supplement your main water supply and irrigate landscapes when there is water scarcity (such as during a drought).

If tanks are not an option, water can still be preserved on the property by being kept in the soil (if the conditions let it) and utilized to resupply the aquifer, which is crucial if you have a well on your property.

Any water that is kept from leaving your property means less water that will wash into the ocean and take various city toxins (oil and rubber from vehicles, dog waste, general trash, etc.). You help clean creeks, streams, rivers, lakes, and seas.

**FUEL.**

Natural gas and propane are two fuels that are frequently used in buildings. They serve various purposes, including powering equipment (such as furnaces, water heaters, clothes dryers, and stoves) and providing comfort and convenience. However, by adopting passive solar architecture, which successfully reduces the amount of fuel used by utilizing the heat from the sun to heat efficiently, and using natural, earthy materials (which benefit from their thermal mass features), some of these pleasures can be built into the structure itself.

As an alternative, various fuel sources can be used, supplied locally from abundantly available resources, and that does not necessitate a difficult extraction process. These are methane digesters, which use composting processes to capture heat.

**POWER.**

Solar power is, of course, the alternative energy source that is most well-known and commonly used. Wind harvesting is the following. Due to the high costs of building power-generating turbines, the spread of wind technology has been relatively gradual thus far.

However, countless others are studying independently and applying different ideas worldwide. Examples of this are gravity-based power generating and wind turbine-free power generation.

**WASTES.**

Structures must "dispose of" a variety of waste streams...

Which are:
- wastewater (from sinks, bathing facilities, and laundry, if present);
- organic materials from food scraps (if a food preparation or consumption use is present in the structure);

Each can be transformed into valuable resources that can be "reinvested" into the site with the correct processing facilities and management systems.

And the advantages of this system are as follows:
- Reduction in the infrastructure needed to transport "wastes" off-site for processing.
- Improved soil microbiology and nutrients.
- Increasing the amount of water accessible to the landscaping plants (which are the best water purifying filters).

## USING PERMACULTURE TO SHAPE THE FUTURE

Since the past year, there has been a sharp increase in awareness of the urgent need for change, which no one can now deny. Most people are beginning to acknowledge the truth of climate change and its relationship to rising droughts, water shortages, and extreme weather events. Each of us has a role to play in finding solutions. A new lexicon, including concepts like "food miles," "footprint," "peak oil," "energy descent," "relocalization," and "water security," is permeating the media and people's consciousness.

For humans and the majority of other species that live on planet earth to have a sustainable future, the current global situation calls for a significant change in how wealthy communities around the world live, think, and expect things to be.

We can no longer afford to use resources at the current rate. Every human being on the planet would require more than 5 (five) plant earth to support themselves if they lived like the average American. We'd need nearly four planets if everyone lived like the average Australian.

Our "Western" way of life truly costs the planet. More resources have been used in the last 30 years than in the previous 200,000 years or the whole history of the human race. In a society that has given in to corporate ambitions and market manipulations at the price of the environment and social justice, notably during the past decade since the mid-1990s, consumerism, economic rationalism, and trade, for trade's sake, have run amok.

We will need to change into a conservative society drastically, overcome our "Affluenza" quickly and smartly, and embrace austerity as a moral imperative if we want to live within our ecological footprint. If we don't become strict with ourselves, the world will become even stricter with us when the costs of inaction or inadequate action begin to mount.

## TAKING CHARGE TO CREATE A SUSTAINABLE FUTURE

In a more significant sense than ever in history, the future is most definitely in our hands. Committing to being an effective steward of the world and assisting others in adjusting to an earth-friendly lifestyle is the most important thing we can do to guide our actions today, tomorrow, and every day after that. We must all learn to live within our means.

This requires us to reinvent ourselves and how we relate to the world around us in all aspects of our daily lives, including our work and the numerous contacts we have with others in our community and society.

While we can do many small things right away by changing our behavior and becoming more conscious consumers, the paradigm shift required to become an effective agent of change necessitates a knowledge, skills, and practical ecological savvy that has been gravely undervalued in our educational systems. There is a lot to learn and not much time to do it.

# Chapter 2:

# Permaculture in the Garden

# CHAPTER 2:
## PERMACULTURE IN THE GARDEN

**B**efore you begin permaculture gardening, could you give it some thought? Determine exactly what a permaculture garden means to you and what you want from it in the first place. Before beginning, you must have at least a basic notion of what you want to build.

You may save time and money by properly designing a permaculture garden. These are the two main reasons why most of us are hesitant to begin a new endeavor, and the most crucial action is taking the time to plan.

You must first decide how your yard will blend into the surrounding surroundings as part of the planning phase. When you've found this out, put nature to work for you. Any garden created using permaculture principles imitates the patterns found in nature. All left is to choose how many concepts you want to use for your garden design.

The project's scope will be partially determined by the size of the garden you choose, and the best part is that it can range from a balcony garden to a fully landscaped yard. Even a little portion of a regular garden can incorporate some permaculture concepts. As with any new gardening technique, it is advisable to begin modestly and develop once you feel confident in your gardening abilities.

After deciding on the size of your new garden, it is time to pick which principles and to what extent you want to apply

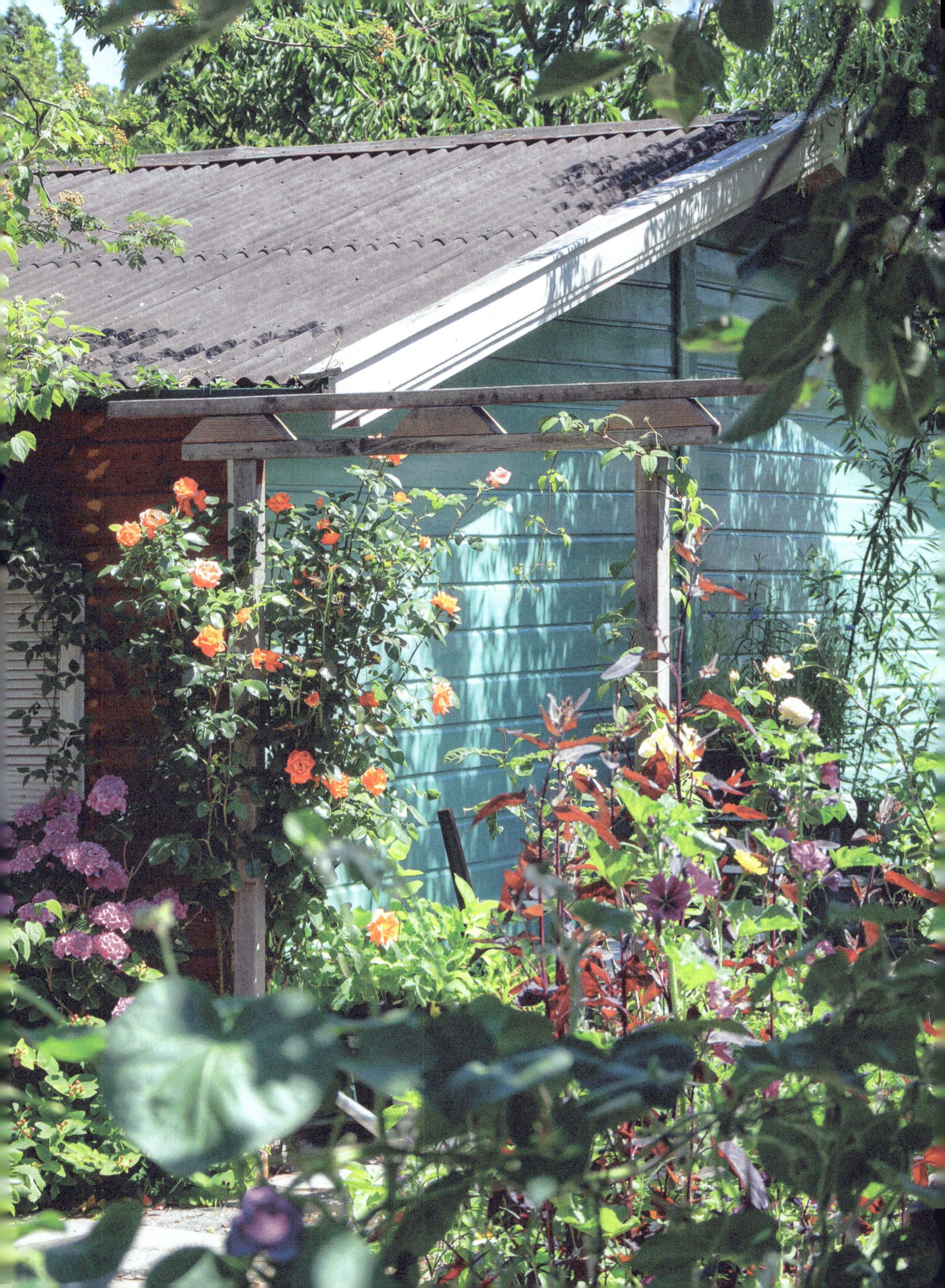

them. All of these rules are inspired by nature. In permaculture gardens, techniques like soil conservation, soil rebuilding, companion planting, plant stacking, succession planting, edge effect, microclimate, vertical gardening, water gardens, monocultures, and polycultures can all be used.

Permaculture gardening is a method of gardening that integrates the best aspects of nature and its wildlife into harmonious wholes. Companion planting, edible landscaping, composting, and native plant culture are just a few techniques that may be used to turn your garden into a low-maintenance, self-contained, productive ecosystem all on its own. These techniques are all ones that nature utilizes naturally in the wild.

A permaculture garden serves numerous purposes and can exist independently of outside influences. A location where a thriving crop is grown, including flowers, herbs, vegetables, and fruit, naturally helps the environment and these plants' health. This self-contained environment is a place that will draw wildlife of all kinds, including insects, mammals, and unseen soil organisms. Each of these species has its advantages and functions.

It's not difficult to create an atmosphere that will look after itself. With a little planning, you can create a healthy garden that will produce thriving vegetables and be good for you and your family. The natural life that works and naturally fertilizes the soil in your garden might be destroyed by using chemicals, which will harm your plants.

Without chemicals, nature has its inventive way of maintaining a clean and safe environment. Our daily gardening activities will help maintain the air we breathe and the water we drink clean if we observe and apply these similar techniques.

Designing a permaculture garden in your yard should consider diversity because nature is all about biodiversity. A successful garden is made up of the right assortment of plants combined in the right way to support one another's growth and boost output.

In addition to being educational, permaculture gardening can be a very gratifying and joyful experience. Watch and take notes on the natural world around your yard to your advantage.

Permaculture in the garden is a holistic approach to designing and managing a garden based on the principles and ethics of Permaculture. It involves creating a garden that mimics natural ecosystems and is self-sustaining and regenerative.

Designing a system resembling natural systems reduces labor and waste, boosts productivity and yields, and restores or preserves the environment. A part of the permaculture whole system approach to living includes gardening.

Permaculture gardening comes naturally in an area as permaculture-rich as Asheville. Due to its popularity, many people in this country have been exposed to it and now follow some or all of its tenets. The most typical technique is to increase the number of perennials and food plants. Our lives become more self-sufficient and less reliant on outside food sources as a result of doing this.

Another typical approach is collecting rainwater runoff in cisterns or barrels to control runoff. Droughts are growing increasingly frequent worldwide, as we all know. Since water is our most valuable resource, collecting rainwater for later use makes sense.

A permaculture system's common fixed elements include the following:
- Continual Gardens (Forest Gardens)
- Catchment Systems for Rain
- Orcharding
- such as chickens, goats, rabbits, and ducks are small agricultural animals.
- Zones
- Guilds

The following are the guiding ideals of Permaculture:
- Don't hurt the earth; take care of it
- Take care of others by assisting and educating one another.
- Limit consumption and distribute excess output to distribute the surplus.

## TECHNIQUES FOR CREATING A PERMACULTURE GARDEN

A method of growing in tune with nature is organic gardening. Growing a profitable, healthy crop in a way that is better for the environment and you.

Producing, harvesting, and preparing your fruits and veggies is exciting, and the health advantages are clear. And while cultivating fruit and vegetables takes up a significant portion of a backyard permaculture system, Permaculture involves much more than just growing food.

Permaculture could be considered a complicated sustainability system, despite not being difficult. Complex in that it makes use of the advantages of an entire system.

Your garden is a very tranquil and relaxing area that may balance a stressed existence in addition to the apparent productive advantages of Permaculture. The beauty and clean air restore one's connection to nature.

# Chapter 3 :

## Permaculture in Agriculture

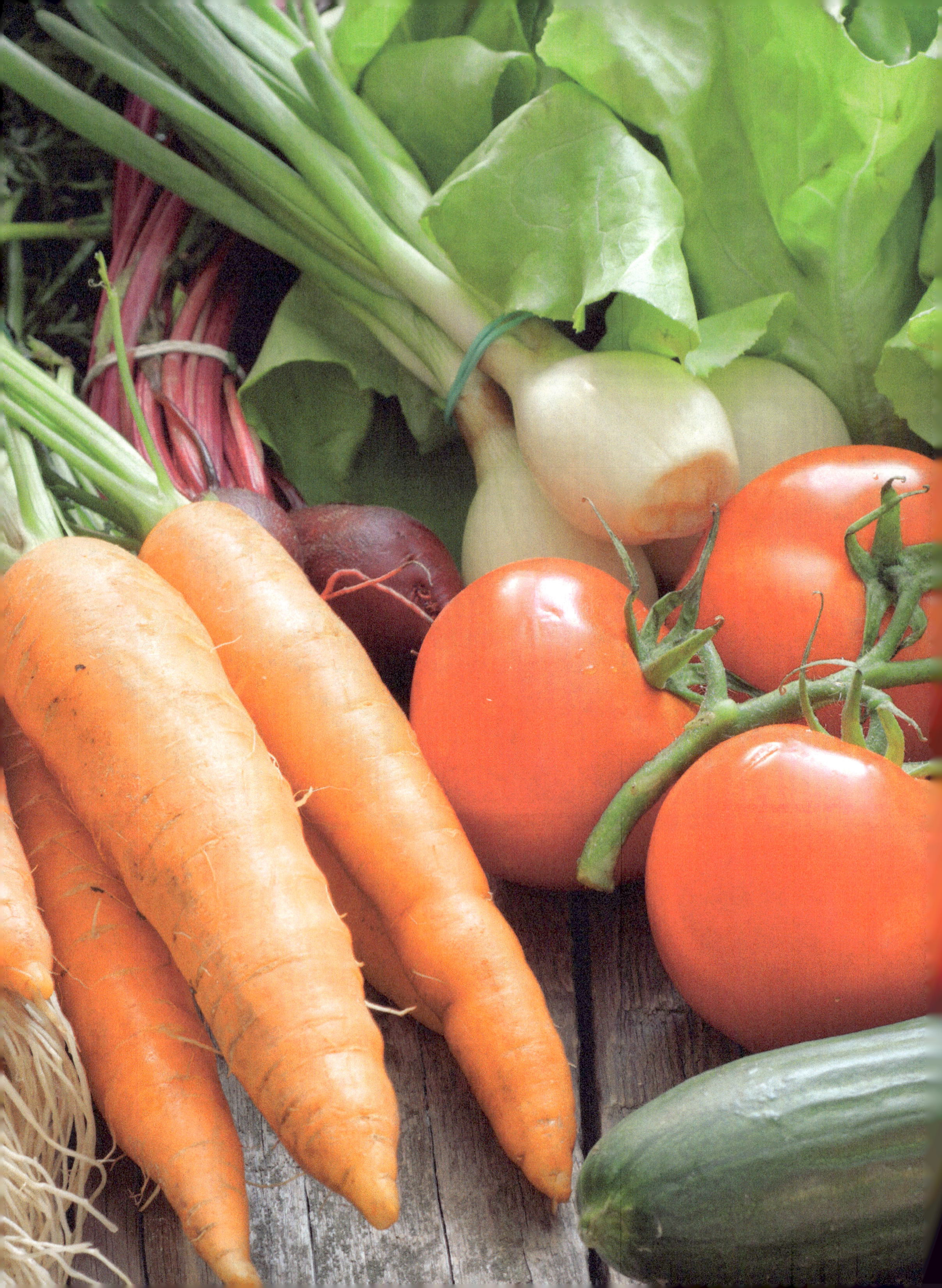

# CHAPTER 3: PERMACULTURE IN AGRICULTURE

The land on which we reside can be used in various ways. Permaculture is the term used to describe sustainable land use planning. This method uses specific designs based on biological and ecological principles that reduce work and maximize results. This is an autonomous farming technique. This system is set up so that it only occasionally or rarely needs human intervention.

Permaculture now refers to a comprehensive strategy for creating human communities that are ecologically balanced and self-sufficient. Permaculture has grown into an international movement right from the start. This idea can be used for all environments and scales, including farms, individual residences, and crowded urban areas.

The goal of this system is to create an ecological equilibrium inside it. A system that is properly balanced doesn't need external adjustments. For instance, a basic permaculture farm feeds its crops with animal excrement, which feeds the animals. The human population is fed simultaneously with enough crops and animal products (such as meat, eggs, etc.).

Permaculture in agriculture is a holistic approach to farming based on the principles and ethics of Permaculture. It involves creating a sustainable and regenerative agricultural system that mimics natural ecosystems and is self-sustaining.

One of the key principles of Permaculture in agriculture is to create a diverse range of plants and animals that work together in a mutually beneficial way. This can include agroforestry, the practice of growing trees and other perennial plants in an agricultural system, and polycultures, the practice of growing multiple crops in the same field. This creates a more resilient and productive system, as the different plants and animals help to maintain soil fertility, control pests, and support biodiversity.

Another important aspect of Permaculture in agriculture is sustainable and regenerative practices. This includes using cover crops and green manures to improve soil health, organic and biodynamic methods to control pests and diseases, and agroecological practices such as crop rotation and intercropping to increase productivity and reduce the need for external inputs.

Permaculture in agriculture also includes rainwater harvesting, swales, and other methods for managing farm water to make the most of rainwater and minimize runoff.

Permaculture in agriculture also includes animal systems, such as chickens, ducks, and other poultry, to control pests, improve soil health, and provide a source of food. Animals can also be managed holistically using methods like rotational grazing, which mimic the natural movement patterns of wild herds and improve soil health.

Permaculture in agriculture also includes the design of the farm as a whole, taking into account the different zones and sectors and the relationships and connections between different elements of the system.

Permaculture in agriculture is a holistic and innovative approach to farming based on the principles and ethics of Permaculture; it creates a sustainable and regenerative agricultural system that supports the health and well-being of the entire ecosystem.

## STRATEGIES FOR CREATING A SUSTAINABLE AND RESILIENT AGRICULTURAL SYSTEM.

Several strategies can be used to create a sustainable and resilient agricultural system, including:

**CROP ROTATION:** Crop rotation is a technique that involves growing different crops in a specific order on the same land, usually every year. This helps to improve soil health, control pests, and reduce the need for external inputs. Crop rotation can also optimize using different resources such as water, light, and nutrients.

**AGROFORESTRY:** Agroforestry is a land-use management system that combines agriculture, forestry, and animal husbandry. It involves growing trees, shrubs, and other perennial plants in an agricultural system, which can provide various benefits, such as reducing erosion, improving soil health, and providing food and other resources. Agroforestry can include practices such as alley cropping, where trees and crops are grown in alternate rows, or silvopasture, which is the practice of grazing animals among trees.

**ANIMAL HUSBANDRY:** Animal husbandry raises and manages animals for food, fiber, or other products. In Permaculture, animals are managed holistically, using methods like rotational grazing, which mimic the natural movement patterns of wild herds and improve soil health. Animals can also be used to control pests, improve soil health, and provide a source of food and other products.

**MULTI-CROPPING:** Multi-cropping is the practice of growing multiple crops in the same field. This creates a more resilient and productive system, as the different crops help to maintain soil fertility, control pests, and support biodiversity. It can also optimize the use of water, light, and nutrients.

**WATER MANAGEMENT:** Water management is essential for sustainable agriculture; it includes techniques such as rainwater harvesting, swales, and other methods for managing water on the farm, to make the most of rainwater and minimize runoff. It also includes the use of contour terracing, the practice of shaping the land to slow water runoff and increase water infiltration.

**SOIL MANAGEMENT:** Soil management is one of the most important aspects of permaculture agriculture; it includes cover crops, green manures, and other methods to improve soil health and fertility. It also includes compost, rock minerals, and other organic matter to improve soil health and fertility.

When implemented, these strategies can create a sustainable and resilient agricultural system that mimics natural ecosystems, is self-sustaining and regenerative, and supports the health and well-being of the entire ecosystem.

## PRODUCTION OF FOOD AND LANDSCAPING

There always appears to be a small piece of earth that needs landscaping care and upkeep, no matter where one life or works. This frequently becomes a hassle or liability in terms of upkeep and appearance. So why not make something that could be a hassle into a benefit?

Any space may be transformed into a highly useful and effective food-producing sanctuary, whether a common area in an apartment building, condominium, gated estate development, commercial campus, or privately held yard or land.

Numerous advantages of this method include:
- Excellent, nutritious food available right outside your kitchen or workplace.
- Safe Food, pesticide- and chemical-free.
- Self-fulfillment and empowerment.
- Rediscovering nature's cycles and seasons.
- Getting to know your community's residents and neighbors.
- Establishing a space and opportunity for education that allows kids to learn about the origins and growth of vegetables like carrots.
- Non-repetitive exercise in the open air boosts brain activity.

## FOR A LANDSCAPING MAKEOVER, USE PERMACULTURE

When it comes to giving your property a makeover, you have lots of options. One set of options has to do with the landscaping your yard receives. What is feasible relies on several variables, including your neighborhood, climate zone, and financial situation. There is also the issue of your personality and how you would go about undergoing such a makeover; you may be an "all or nothing" type, or you may like to take things slowly, one step at a time.

We'll examine a concept that costs you nothing, offers a potential framework for your design ideas, and introduce a long list of queries to help you get started on your thought process. The concept is zonation, taken from the sustainable living method called "permaculture."

It encourages you to create "zones"—or activity areas—on your land. There could be up to five zones on a suburban lot, though you can have less if it works better for your situation. Every region has a dominant activity pattern and a dominant type of productive plant life.

**Zone 1** is the region you frequent the most, including any patios or decks where you spend most of your outdoor time and the vicinity of the entrances and exits you use the most frequently. These are your main areas for entertainment and relaxation. Herbs, salad plants, strawberries, and tomatoes in season are among the plantings you might want to grab quickly for the kitchen in this zone.

A little farther out from the house lies the second zone, and a grassy area for the kids to play may be included. This location allows you to grow perennial shrubs and berrying canes (raspberries, currants); these plants need minimal maintenance.

The third zone is the primary production zone for those who enjoy growing their food. Brassicas (such as cabbage, kale, broccoli, and others), potatoes, sweet potatoes, corn, and other crops will be grown in these beds, along with fruit trees, including apples, peaches, and pears. The opportunity exists for cleverly planned walkways in this area to unexpectedly disclose a "secret" pocket of unique delights, such as a concealed water feature, a blaze of spring, summer, or fall color, or a skillfully constructed sculpture. Families may find the third zone useful for kids to burn off energy playing hide-and-seek or to use play structures like swings, slides, or trampolines.

There may be room for a fourth zone on many suburban sites. This includes plantings that entice birds to visit your garden or settle there. Here, larger flowering trees like rhododendrons or magnolias can grow. This area may also have larger nut-bearing trees (walnuts, macadamias, and the like). Dedicated vegetable growers can use hedge or shrubbery screens to conceal their compost containers. Depending on local laws, you might even think about the advantages of a small livestock unit. How appealing is a newly hatched egg?

Your available land may appear larger than it is by using zones. It makes your yard more adaptable and offers significantly more interest than is achievable with a monoculture of mowed grass.

## SYSTEMS OF ANIMALS.

Today, the only animals in our lives are pets, and everything beyond that is quite mysterious. However, several towns are altering their rules to permit the entrance of animal systems (even on a small scale).

Bees and chickens stand out as the creatures that seem to intrude on our life the most. And it is not by chance that it is them; in reality, not only do they both produce savory and nourishing products like honey and eggs, but they are also devoted companions. That is what they naturally do, and the fact that their actions improve our lives is purely coincidental. Bees pollinate plants, without which most of our food would not grow, and chickens improve soil fertility and raise the quality of the food we grow.

A wealth of material is accessible to research these complex topics in depth. They were briefly described here to give an overview of what is possible and to share the thrill of the possibilities hidden inside each project.

This can lead to a series of articles that expand on each subject.

This is what permaculture design does—it sets up every system component to run as efficiently as possible by exploiting naturally occurring patterns and functions. It provides backup systems where many elements can carry out the same function and stacking functions, ensuring that each element can handle multiple tasks.

At first, all of this information may seem overwhelming, so it is crucial to plan for each system carefully. Don't overlook the exciting prospects open to you if you plan a building project, an addition, or a remodel of your house or company.

## NATURE GARDENING IN YOUR BACKYARD USING PERMACULTURE

A gardening technique known as Permaculture is based on ecological and biological concepts. It is a natural style of gardening that collaborates with nature to maximize the available resources for plant growth while simultaneously reducing the amount of physical labor required to produce a flourishing garden.

One of the nicest things about permaculture gardening is that it can be scaled to any size and adapted to any setting, including rural, suburban, and urban regions. The concepts of Permaculture can be used in landscaping and container gardens, as well as window boxes and all other traditional gardening techniques.

You will need to understand ecological systems and the theory behind Permaculture to implement it into your gardening methods and foster a healthy environment. Every component of a permaculture system should be advantageous to the system, and the interactions between these components should work to support it. The state of the land you are growing your crops on will be improved, productivity will be maximized, and the land will be used indefinitely with a well-designed system with positive connections between the elements.

To do this, recycle animal, plant, or other permaculture system waste so that it can be used to benefit another element of the system, as nature would naturally do. The greatest method to learn how an ecosystem is formed is to study how nature behaves naturally in your region. Without the need to artificially add nutrients to the soil, the mechanism by which they are refilled back into the system is natural. This is a means of avoiding pollution in addition to being cost-effective.

Contrary to normal agricultural systems, which produce large quantities of a single crop, diversity is a key component of Permaculture. In Permaculture, several types of plants and animals complement one another. In this manner, there is a fair probability that within the system, if a predator or insect attacks any one species, a natural defense mechanism will be in place to protect it or defend it before the crop is affected. In contemporary agriculture, a crop can be destroyed if a pest attacks it.

It is easy to get much more out of life by consuming less if you carefully consider how we use our resources, energy, food, material and non-material requirements, and housing. By using permaculture techniques, you may increase your output while exerting less work, benefiting the environment and ourselves both now and in the future.

A healthy and environmentally beneficial method of gardening. A method of growing in tune with nature is organic gardening. Growing a profitable, healthy crop in a way that is better for the environment and you.

# Chapter 4:
## Water Managemeny in Permaculture

# CHAPTER 4: WATER MANAGEMENT IN PERMACULTURE

**W**ater management is an essential aspect of Permaculture, as it plays a critical role in the health and productivity of the ecosystem. Permaculture water management techniques are based on capturing, storing, and using water efficiently and mimicking natural water cycles.

Some key techniques of water management in Permaculture include:

**RAINWATER HARVESTING:** Rainwater harvesting involves capturing and storing rainwater using rain barrels or cisterns or creating swales and other earthworks that slow and store water on the landscape. Rainwater harvesting allows water to be collected and stored during dry periods.

**GREYWATER RECYCLING:** This involves reusing water from sinks, showers, and laundry for irrigation, flushing toilets, and other non-potable uses. Greywater recycling can reduce the demand for fresh water and help to conserve resources.

**SWALES:** Swales are shallow trenches that slow and store water on a landscape. They are typically dug along contour lines and are lined with a permeable material to increase water infiltration. Swales can help to reduce erosion, improve soil health, and increase water availability.

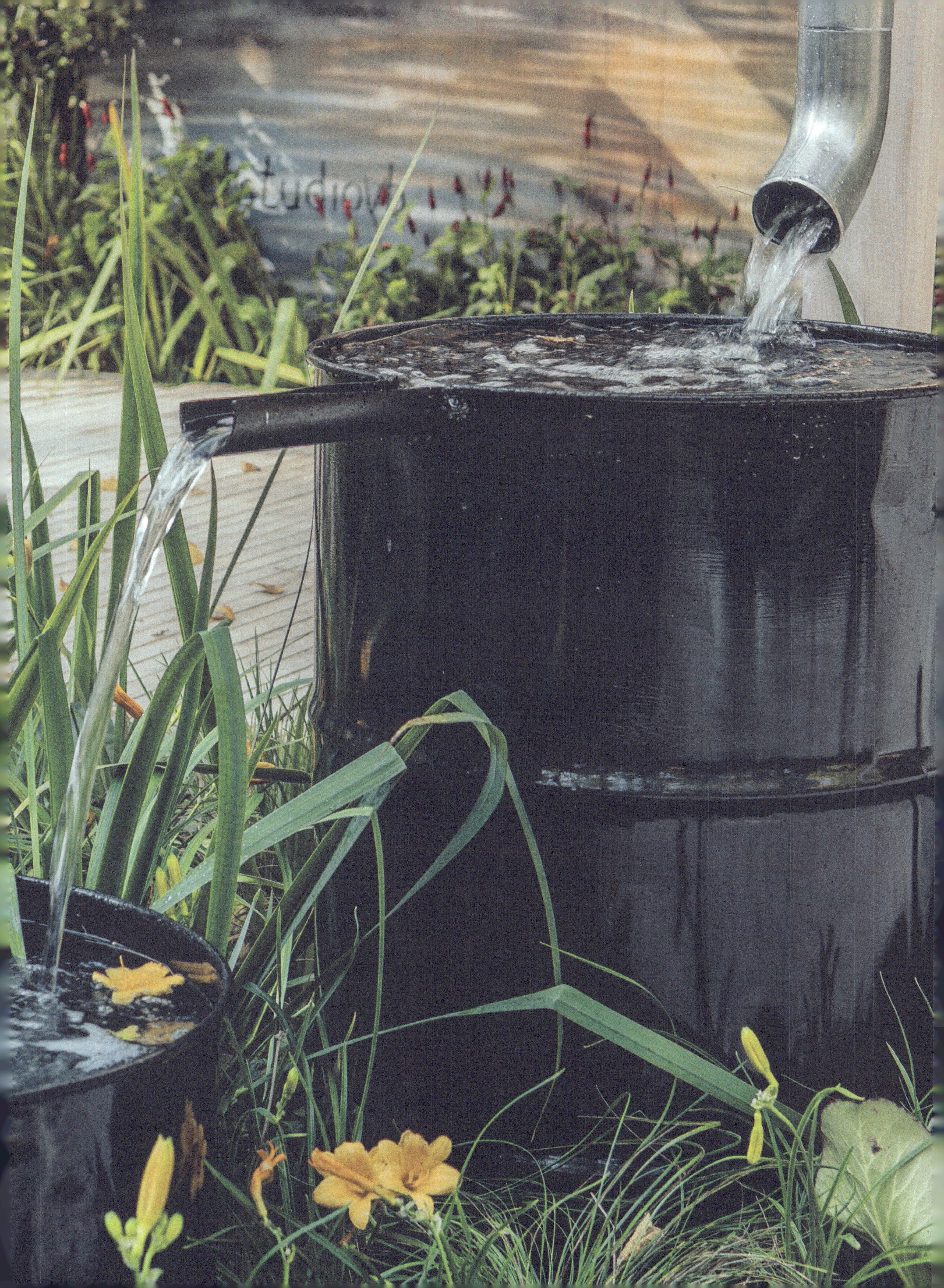

**EARTHWORKS:** Earthworks include techniques such as terracing, which shapes the land to slow water runoff and increase water infiltration. Earthworks can help to reduce erosion, improve soil health, and increase water availability.

**MULCHING:** Mulching covers the soil with organic material to retain moisture and suppress weeds. Mulch helps to reduce evaporation, improve soil health and fertility, and increase water availability.

**MICRO-CATCHMENT:** Micro-catchment systems are small-scale water harvesting structures built on sloping land to catch and store rainwater for later use. It includes techniques like contour bunds, keyline systems, and micro-dams.

Permaculture water management involves capturing, storing, and using water efficiently and mimicking natural water cycles. It includes rainwater harvesting, greywater recycling, swales, earthworks, mulching, and micro-catchment. These techniques can help conserve resources and increase water availability in the ecosystem.

## TECHNIQUES FOR CAPTURING, STORING, AND USING WATER IN A PERMACULTURE SYSTEM.

In Permaculture, water is viewed as a precious resource that should be captured, stored, and used efficiently. Several techniques can be used to capture, store, and use water in a permaculture system, including:

**RAINWATER HARVESTING:** Rainwater harvesting involves capturing and storing rainwater, either by using rain barrels or cisterns or by creating swales and other earthworks that slow and store water on the landscape. Rainwater harvesting allows water to be collected and stored during dry periods. This can include simple techniques such as installing a gutter and downspout system to collect rainwater from a roof and directing it into a cistern or more complex systems like creating a pond or lake to store water.

**GREYWATER RECYCLING:** This involves reusing water from sinks, showers, and laundry for irrigation, flushing toilets, and other non-potable uses. Greywater recycling can reduce the demand for fresh water and help to conserve resources. This can include simple techniques such as diverting greywater from sinks and showers to a nearby garden or more complex systems like using a greywater treatment system to purify and reuse the water.

**IRRIGATION METHODS:** Several irrigation methods can be used in Permaculture, including drip irrigation, which delivers water directly to the roots of plants, and sub-irrigation, which delivers water through the soil or porous material. Mulching can also retain moisture in the soil and reduce the need for irrigation.

**EARTHWORKS:** Earthworks include techniques such as terracing, which shapes the land to slow water runoff and increase water infiltration. Earthworks can help to reduce erosion, improve soil health, and increase water availability. This can include building terrace walls to slow water runoff and increase water infiltration or creating swales to slow and store water on the landscape.

**MICRO-CATCHMENT SYSTEMS:** Micro-catchment systems are small-scale water harvesting structures built on sloping land to catch and store rainwater for later use. It includes techniques like contour bunds, keyline systems, and micro-dams.

Techniques for capturing, storing, and using water in a permaculture system include rainwater harvesting, greywater recycling, irrigation methods, earthworks, and micro-catchment systems. These techniques can help conserve resources and increase water availability in the ecosystem.

# Chapter 5 : Energy and Climate in Permaculture

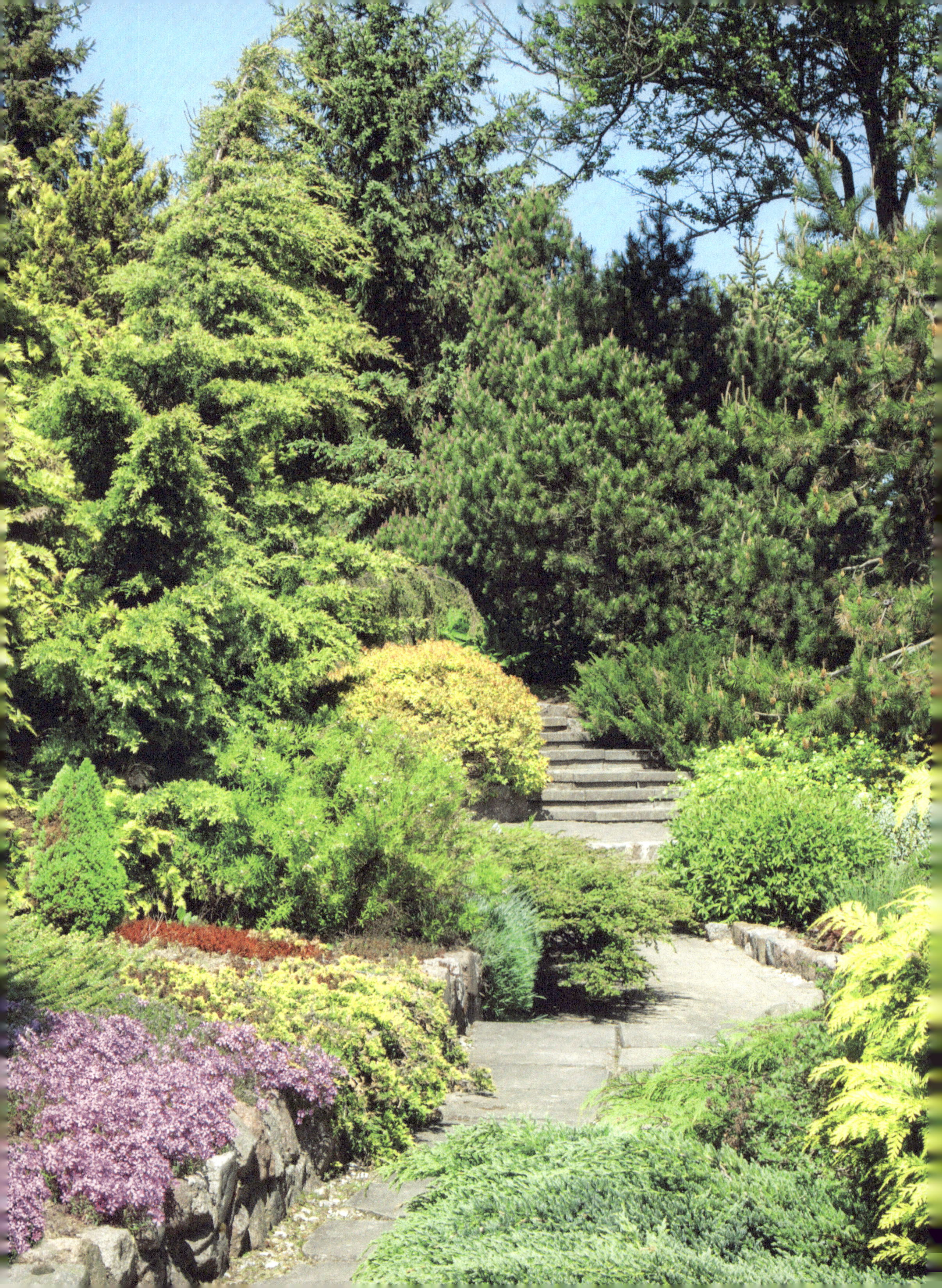

# CHAPTER 5:
# ENERGY AND CLIMATE IN PERMACULTURE

Energy and climate are important considerations in Permaculture, as they play a critical role in the health and productivity of the ecosystem. Permaculture design principles and strategies can be used to create a more energy-efficient and climate-resilient system.

**ENERGY EFFICIENCY:** Permaculture design principles can create more energy-efficient systems, such as incorporating energy-efficient building design, using renewable energy sources, and reducing energy consumption through energy-saving technologies and practices.

**RENEWABLE ENERGY:** Permaculture systems can incorporate renewable energy sources such as solar, wind, and hydropower. These sources can provide a sustainable and reliable energy source, reducing dependence on fossil fuels.

**PASSIVE COOLING AND HEATING:** Permaculture design principles can be used to create buildings and structures that are naturally cooled and heated through techniques such as passive solar design, earth sheltering, and thermal mass.

**CLIMATE-RESILIENT AGRICULTURE:** Permaculture strategies such as agroforestry, crop rotation, and intercropping can create a more climate-resilient agricultural system. These techniques can help increase crops' resilience to changing weather conditions and reduce the impacts of climate change on agricultural production.

**BIODIVERSITY:** Permaculture design principles can create a more biodiverse ecosystem, which can help increase the system's resilience to changing climate conditions. This can include incorporating a diverse range of plants and animals and creating habitats that support biodiversity.

Permaculture design principles and strategies can be used to create a more energy-efficient, climate-resilient, and biodiverse system. This can include incorporating renewable energy sources, passive cooling and heating, climate-resilient agriculture, and biodiversity. These strategies, when implemented together, can help reduce human activity's impact on the climate and create a more sustainable and resilient future for humanity and the planet.

## STRATEGIES FOR REDUCING ENERGY CONSUMPTION AND MITIGATING THE IMPACTS OF CLIMATE CHANGE IN A PERMACULTURE SYSTEM.

Several strategies can be used to reduce energy consumption and mitigate the impacts of climate change in a permaculture system, including:

**RENEWABLE ENERGY:** Incorporating renewable energy sources such as solar, wind, and hydropower can provide a sustainable and reliable energy source and reduce dependence on fossil fuels. This can include using solar panels, wind turbines, or micro-hydro systems to generate electricity or using solar water heaters, cookers, and other renewable energy technologies to reduce energy consumption.

**PASSIVE SOLAR DESIGN:** This technique is used to harness the energy from the sun to heat and cool buildings. This can include using south-facing windows, thermal mass, and natural ventilation to heat buildings in the winter and shading and natural ventilation to cool buildings in the summer.

**INSULATION:** Proper insulation can reduce energy consumption for heating and cooling buildings. This can include using insulation made from natural materials such as cellulose, wool, or cotton or using insulated concrete forms to build more energy-efficient buildings.

**ENERGY-EFFICIENT APPLIANCES AND LIGHTING:** Using energy-efficient appliances can reduce energy consumption. This can include using LED light bulbs, energy Star-rated appliances, and other energy-saving technologies.

**GREEN TRANSPORTATION:** Encouraging green transportation such as cycling, walking, and public transportation can reduce energy consumption and help mitigate the impacts of climate change.

**SUSTAINABLE BUILDING MATERIALS:** Using sustainable building materials such as bamboo, rammed earth, or cob can reduce energy consumption and mitigate the impacts of climate change.

**EFFICIENT WATER USAGE:** Efficient water usage, such as rainwater harvesting, greywater recycling, and drip irrigation, can reduce energy consumption and mitigate the impacts of climate change.

Several strategies can be used to reduce energy consumption and mitigate the impacts of climate change in a permaculture system, including incorporating renewable energy sources, passive solar design, insulation, energy-efficient appliances and lighting, green transportation, sustainable building materials, and efficient water usage. These strategies, when implemented together, can help to reduce the impact of human activity on the climate and create a more sustainable and resilient future for humanity

# Chapter 6 :
# Permaculture in the Community

# CHAPTER 6:
## PERMACULTURE IN THE COMMUNITY

The permaculture idea is practiced worldwide, although it is especially popular in developing nations. People without communities are taught how to live off the land's natural resources. For communities to become self-sufficient, natural water systems, wastewater treatment systems, and land stewardship education are designed and taught.

Several inner-city neighborhoods are embracing Permaculture in the United States to restore sustainable communities. There are several model permaculture communities, one in Brooklyn, New York, has a program to teach young people how to be sustainable farmers in addition to community gardens, a beekeeping business, a chicken and egg program, and a chicken and egg program. They offer consultation to other communities interested in developing their permaculture systems. It is an amazing program.

Permaculture in the community is an approach that uses permaculture design principles and strategies to create sustainable, resilient, and regenerative communities. It focuses on creating social, economic, and ecological systems that are interconnected and mutually supportive.

### STRATEGIES FOR CREATING PERMACULTURE COMMUNITIES

Some key strategies for creating permaculture communities include:

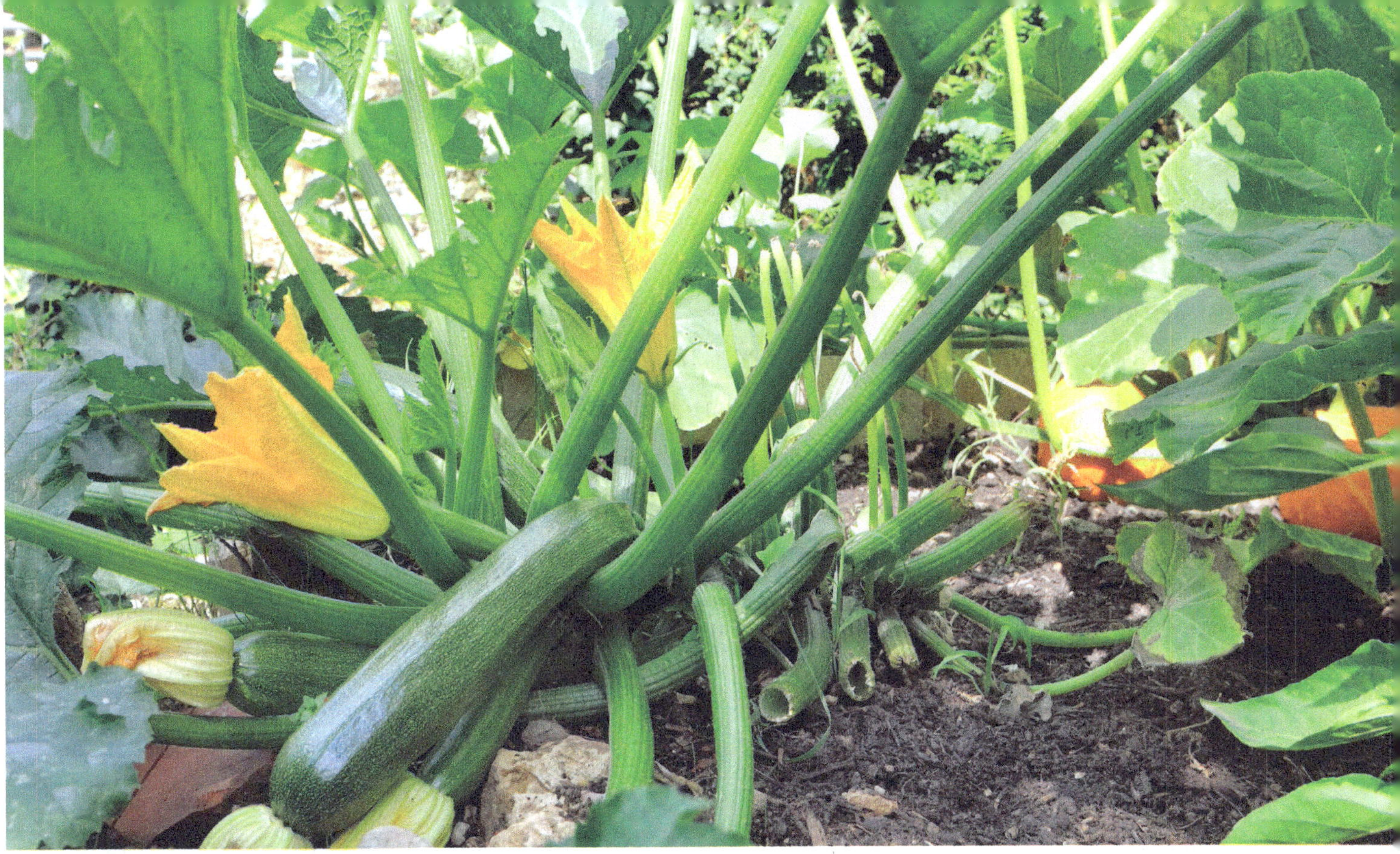

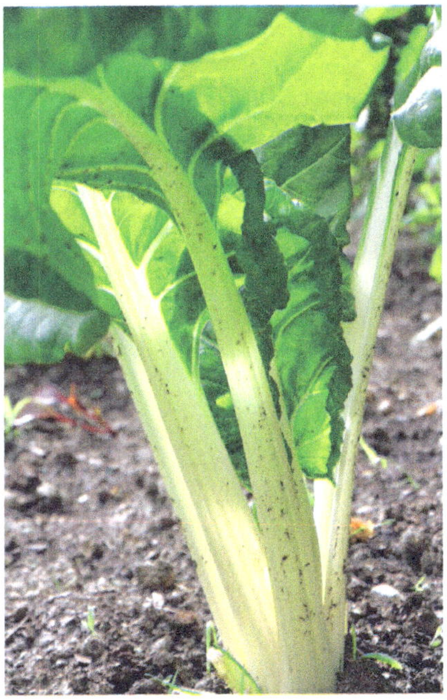

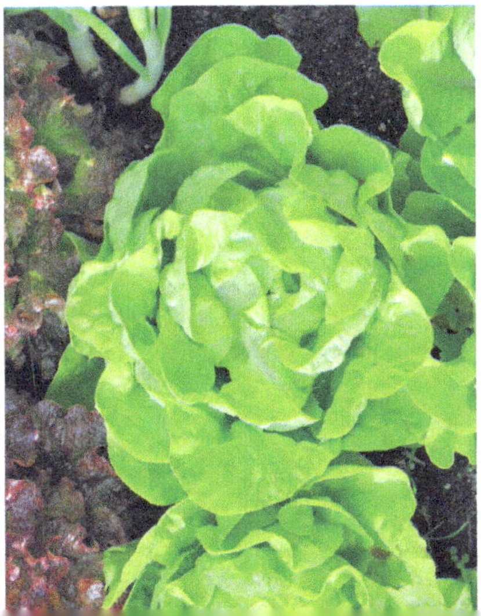

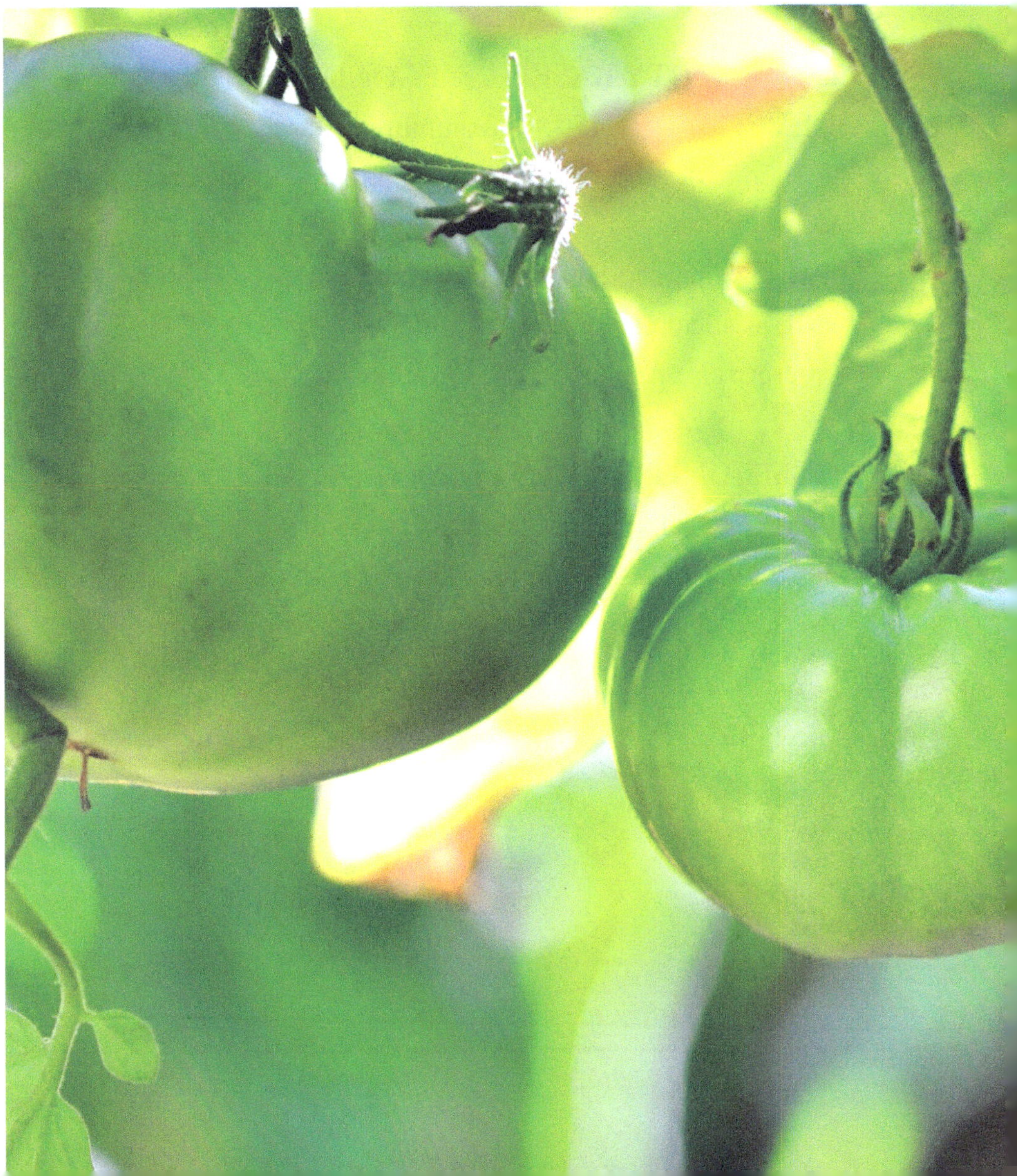

**COMMUNITY GARDENING AND URBAN AGRICULTURE:** Community gardening and urban agriculture can create local food systems that provide healthy, fresh, and affordable food for the community. This can include community gardens, rooftop gardens, and other forms of urban agriculture.

**NATURAL BUILDING:** Natural building is an approach that uses sustainable and locally sourced materials to construct buildings that are energy-efficient, healthy, and durable. This can include techniques such as cob, straw bale, and rammed earth construction.

**COMMUNITY-BASED ECONOMIC DEVELOPMENT:** Community-based economic development can be used to create local economies that are resilient, equitable, and sustainable. This can include strategies such as local currencies, community-owned enterprises, and worker cooperatives.

**COMMUNITY RESILIENCE AND PREPAREDNESS:** Community resilience and preparedness are important aspects of Permaculture in the community; it includes strategies such as building community resilience to natural disasters, emergencies, and other disruptions, as well as community-wide planning to prepare for potential disruptions.

**COMMUNITY EDUCATION AND ENGAGEMENT:** Community education and engagement are key components of Permaculture in the community. It includes educating and empowering community members to become active participants in creating sustainable and resilient communities and engaging with community members to build shared vision and goals.

Techniques for creating a resilient and sustainable community include community gardens, shared resources, and cooperative living.

# Chapter 7 : Natural Building in Permaculture

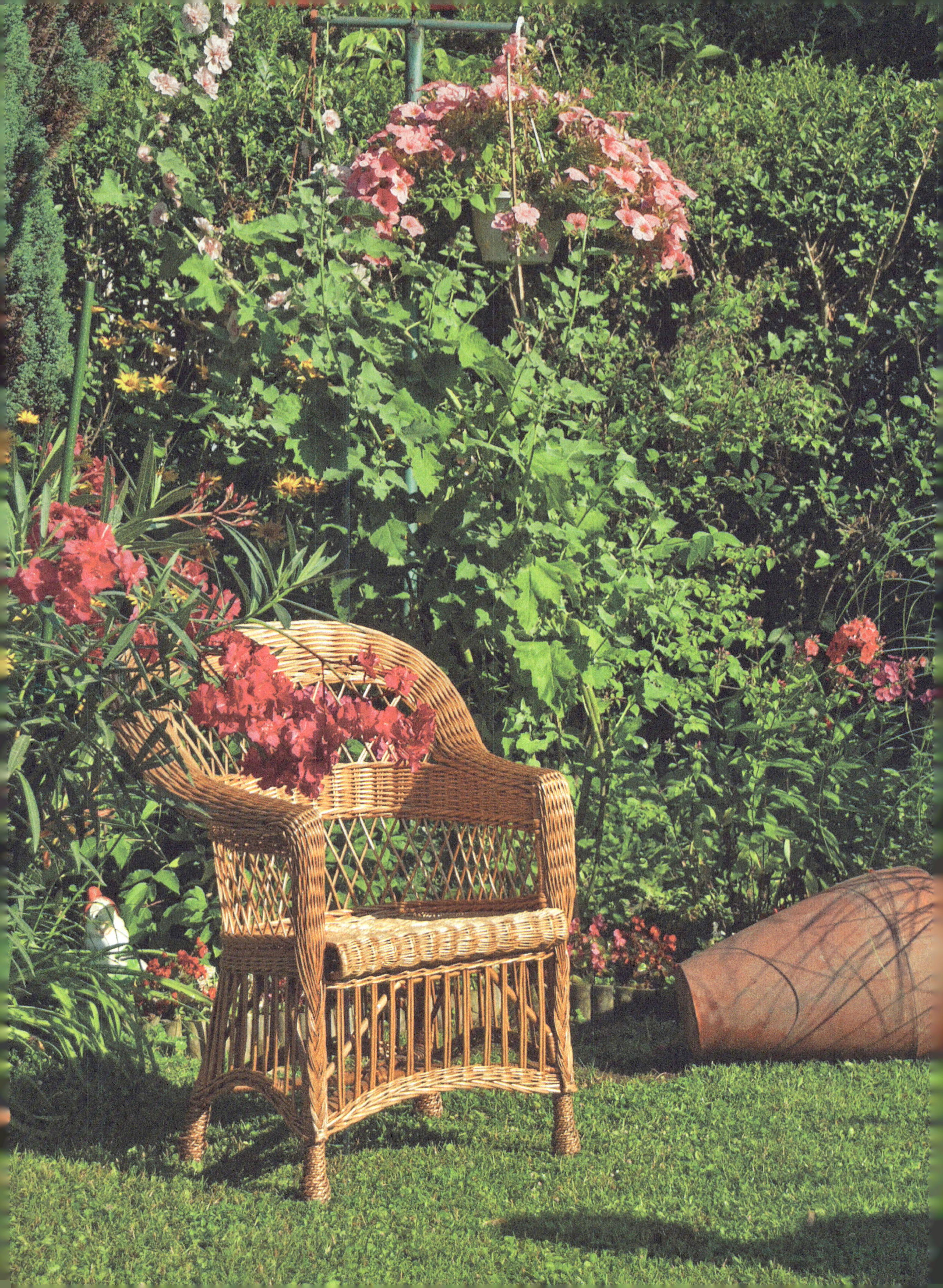

# CHAPTER 7:
# NATURAL BUILDING IN PERMACULTURE

**P**ermaculture is based on observation and planning. Before constructing a farm, one must observe, research, and comprehend its natural components and how they interact. The system's boundaries, both natural and artificial, and the natural resources that are accessible within it must both be taken into account.

Evaluating these parameters then influences the design, execution, and maintenance of the permaculture system. The system's success depends on the design, a highly original and creative process.

One of the design's main elements is using natural patterns (such as waves or spirals, which are frequent) and patterns beneficial for a specific requirement (like a particular structure to minimize waste).

Permaculture frequently uses layers to organize space in a way that is both harmonious and effective. For instance, layering several plant sizes on a single soil patch can maximize space consumption and enable the emergence of a diversified and complementary ecosystem.

Communities have been successful in converting vacant sites into greenhouses and gardens. Vegetables can be grown even in small backyards, and each neighbor can grow one or two varieties of fruit, vegetables, or herbs, giving the neighborhood a wide selection to share and sell.

A single backyard has been created, fostering not only the establishment of a garden but also the collaboration of residents living as active members of the neighborhood. On top of buildings, water collecting systems have been created to utilize the water in the gardens. On a social as well as an ecological level, it is genuinely bridging gaps.

The neighborhood gardens stand to gain in several ways. In many cases, it's the only method for local seniors to receive fresh produce and fruits for less money. Teaching parents how to buy and cook fresh foods for their families is a priceless opportunity. Children can learn the value of eating wholesome foods grown on the ground from the gardens.

Many people who rent apartments are growing herbs to go with bigger, more sustainable gardens. It promotes the objective of consuming wholesome foods devoid of many additives. Even apartments can install solar panels to save energy, and anyone can participate.

This idea also applies to community developers creating places based on the earth and people. It plans communal gardens right in the heart of city districts and practical alternative transit systems, bike lanes, and pedestrian trails. It is a dedication to the whole community, which is feasible and sustainable.

It has evolved into a company. There are edible container gardens, backyard tier-garden systems, and gardens in a bag for sale. That is evidence of the permaculture movement's expansion.

Terms like integrated farming, ecological engineering, and cultivated ecology convey the same concept. The permaculture movement seeks to restore the ability of the soil to sustain towns, villages, and families in their natural state.

The communal garden could be the catalyst for the collective dinner. It transitions to bicycle commuting, greenhouse construction in metropolitan areas, and solar panel installation to lessen dependency on depleting energy sources rather than restoring them.

## TECHNIQUES FOR CREATING STRUCTURES THAT ARE IN HARMONY WITH THE ENVIRONMENT

Various structural components and sustainable building materials are used in natural buildings. Natural building techniques that promote sustainability emphasize robustness and the use of easily accessible, abundant, or renewable resources, as well as those that, when recycled or salvaged, create healthy living spaces and preserve indoor air quality. Natural construction typically relies more on manual labor than on technology. It is dependent upon the regional environment, geology, and climate, the characteristics of the particular building site, and the requirements and personalities of the creators and users.

Natural building is based on reducing the environmental impact of structures and other supporting systems without compromising convenience or well-being. Natural building is more environmentally friendly because it primarily uses readily available, renewable, reusable, or recycled materials. Rapidly renewable resources are being used more and more. The emphasis on architectural design is increased in addition to using natural building materials. Fundamentally, operational costs are reduced, and the environment is improved by a building's orientation, use of the local climate and site conditions, and design emphasis on natural ventilation. Compact construction and reducing environmental impact are prevalent, as are on-site energy management, on-site water capture, alternative sewage treatment, and water reuse.

## DEVELOPING PATTERN

Two distinct development tendencies in the sport have emerged between industrialized and developing nations. People in highly developed places have fully embraced modern society and its material blessings, but they have also started to experience the negative effects of over-exploitation. Thus, some of them have started to consider and consider the impact of the industrial revolution and modern living on all of human society. Return to life, learn from nature, and lead a basic and laborious life by returning to the living environment and even the influence of personal life. On the other hand, in regions with slow growth, the mainstream value is still more cost-effective, even though it still reflects the widespread desire for material civilization. People have looked to ancient knowledge, the earth's natural resources, and conventional methods of reform or innovation to find ways to improve current living conditions in poor, unqualified areas that have supported the development of modern science and technology and the industrialization of architecture.

## NATURAL MATERIAL

It is not because the natural building movement is a novel and innovative architectural approach, nor is it to build more structures; rather, it is to serve as a general daily practice for all areas of food and clothing. By becoming a part of it, you represent the purpose and value of a simple life, the pursuit, and discovery of life itself, and looking into potential alternate locations for human habitation. I believe that living a simple, natural life is doable. Environmentally speaking, it is not required to create structures that stand the test of time but to fundamentally self-cleanse the building and its associated activities. When a structure reaches the end of its life cycle or when people depart the planet, it does not contaminate the environment or leave as much trash behind as possible. In essence, it is unnecessary to address environmental issues if living can be natural and straightforward. Life is contained in buildings. The themes of architectural design and construction are all the space and amenities required to satisfy all activities in life. As a result, natural buildings are considered just the buildings themselves, including the surrounding land and any necessary living amenities.

## ESSENTIAL GUIDELINES

In a broad sense, natural architecture includes various potential materials and techniques. The only standard that needs to be followed is whether the adopted techniques require the least energy and environmental impact when using material resources. The environmental impact is negligible. Use local and natural resources as much as possible while choosing materials, keeping in mind that local materials are typically preferred. The least processed materials should be utilized whenever possible, and recycled resources should be extensively used. Before building, it is vital to gather and correctly store the supplies gradually. The major power tools used in the construction process are labor and hand tools, with little to no use of power tools. Home builders must evaluate the construction technique based on specific circumstances. The technical bar is modest in theory. Individuals may easily begin most of the task, which is the primary criterion for evaluation.

In order to meet the demands of modern life, some of the fundamental application methods for energy use include creating a cycle of materials and energy, such as composting kitchen waste, dry and wet separated composting toilets, rainwater, and Zhongshui; and fusing renewable energy technologies, such as solar thermal, solar photovoltaic, and wind. Garbage is lost as waste and pollution because there are only so many resources on the planet; however, recycling turns waste into a resource that may be utilized indefinitely.

Due to individuals, periods, and places, natural buildings may have diverse options and practices. Both standards and non-standards are relative concepts. However, every component of a person's makeup will be recycled after they no longer require a building. In addition to the industrialized materials, they should be able to naturally restore the composition that was before they left the land and return to the natural cycle.

Additionally, recycled industrial materials should not utilize energy or get contaminated during recycling if they are utilized. For instance, although the soil is a common component of land, it must undergo a protracted geological process to form, and arable land is only spread over a small surface in a particular region. As a possible use for such valuable earth in construction: First, whether the soil can still be easily sorted out at the end of its life cycle to return to the pastoral or enter the garbage landfill as part of building materials; second, whether the restored soil of the picture-perfect countryside is as pure as ever and suitable for planting wholesome crops with confidence.

This activity, where physical labor and spiritual creativity are the main focuses of life, is a desire for a clean life and life, an effort to revive the tradition of independence and cooperation, and the creation of teachers and methods to carry on the architectural knowledge and traditional artisans' skills of the ancestors and seek further. To meet the demands of modern people for aesthetics and living quality, research and development, combining suitable environmental protection technology and technology with creativity to develop the qualities of natural materials and recycled materials in the earth, establish a material and energy circulation system, and can provide traditional materials, construction methods, Technology's new life are fit for modern life and the ultimate goal of peaceful cohabitation between people and the environment. Therefore, the conventional architectural framework can be used without restriction, even though a large portion of natural buildings draw strength from traditional ways of construction. It is full of several kinds of practice, as long as the homebuilder's imagination and capacity will allow. It may be said that the possibility is a very experimental structure.

Natural design is based on the idea that one should only take what is necessary and build the spaces required for survival. Even if natural or recycled materials are utilized for building above this point, another type of waste will be added under the heading of natural construction. The most appropriate engineering and technology for the local climate, way of life, availability of labor, and material circumstances will be produced in various locations throughout human history to satisfy current residential needs.

On the one hand, the development potential of natural architecture calls for the return of old wisdom to everyday life and construction. It is a construction philosophy and technique characterized by kindness, localization, manual work, tenderness, and goodwill toward the environment and all living things, including humans. Technology is environmentally friendly while providing modern life's necessities for convenience, beauty, functionality, and safety. This makes an area that modern people are content to live in, which subsequently improves the appearance of modern living and makes it appear more cozy and organic.

The ecological construction movement has grown for decades on a global scale. The "back to nature" movement might still fall short of offering a solution for the sustainable survival of humanity. But despite its best efforts, it has resisted industrialization over the years. Another approach is deciding to live.

**STUDYING AND EXERCISING**

For fixed-point bases that are self-directed homebuilders, curious hobbyists, or those looking to invest in professional activities, professional courses are frequently offered. Among these, professional development programs frequently include on-site internships. After the training, teachers are sent to different locations to work alongside seasoned experts to continue honing their abilities until they are independent. In addition to their capacity to seek self-education to have a leading project, inexperienced self-created homebuilders frequently invite experts to open classes on their property.

**MATERIALS**

Sand and clay are materials used in many different kinds of natural buildings. The combination can create a cob or adobe when combined with water and typically straw or another fiber (clay blocks). Earth (as rammed earth or earth bags), wood (cordwood or timber frame/post-and-beam), straw, rice hulls, bamboo, and stone are frequently utilized in natural architecture. In natural buildings, various recycled or reused non-toxic materials, such as urbanite (recycled concrete fragments), auto windscreens, and other recycled glass, are frequently employed.

Practitioners of this building method avoid utilizing other materials because of their major negative impacts on the environment or human health. These include paints and other coatings that emit volatile organic compounds (VOCs), steel, and some plastics, especially polyvinyl chloride (PVC or "vinyl"), and those containing harmful plasticizers or hormone-mimicking formulations. Waste materials include rubber tires in recycling areas, unsustainable wood harvesting, toxic wood preservatives, and mixes based on Portland cement.

**TECHNIQUES**

A lot of time-tested methods and supplies are enjoying a rebirth in favor. Based on local material availability and climate-appropriate building design, this varies globally.

**ADOBE**

Adobe, one of the oldest construction techniques, is merely clay and sand mixed with water. For increased robustness, chopped straws or other fibers are frequently used. The final step is to let the mixture dry in the appropriate shape. Adobe is typically formed into bricks that may be piled to create walls.

Several statements are made regarding the ideal ratios of clay and sand (or larger aggregate). Some claim that 15% to 30% clay binds the material together and is present in the best adobe soil. Others contend that the greatest mixture for preventing brick cracking or fragmentation is one with an equal amount of clay and sand. The blocks can either be pressed into blocks or poured into molds and dried. Adobe flooring is aesthetically pleasing and durable since it is colored with clay and polished with natural oil.

Adobe structures often feature substantial foundations and broad overhanging eaves to protect the walls and minimize maintenance. For appearance and protection, adobe can be plastered with cob- or lime-based mixtures. Because Adobe has a high thermal mass, it conducts heat and cold slowly. As a result, insulation can be added, ideally on the exterior, or a double wall with insulation or a gap in between can be constructed. The conventional, heavy, uninsulated adobe works well in areas with mild winters or where the predictable daily sun is present during those cold months.

## COB

A monolithic building system made of a combination of clay, sand, straw, and earth is referred to as a cob. The building is constructed entirely from the ground up without using forms, bricks, or a timber framework. The usage of various "mud" building techniques dates back at least 10,000 years and has been practiced in many regions of the world for generations.

Before the 13th century, cob construction was used in England. It declined in popularity after World War I but is currently seeing a comeback. Despite being one of the most labor-intensive building techniques, cob is also one of the simplest and least expensive. The adaptability of cob is another big benefit; it is simple to mold into any shape. Even though cob construction was becoming less popular in England by the late 19th century, hundreds of cob structures remain today (20,000 in Devon, England alone). Today, between one-third and fifty percent of the world's population are thought to reside in huts made of earth. Although it is often associated with "low-rise" buildings, it has been utilized for centuries in Yemen and other Middle-Eastern nations in "apartment" buildings of eight stories or more.

Adobe, earth bags, timber frames, cordwood, and straw bales are a few natural building techniques using cob-like materials such as plaster or filling. Earth is, therefore, a key component in natural construction.

## CORDWOOD

"cordwood construction" refers to a natural building technique in which short lengths of debarked tree pieces are built up crosswise with mortar or cob mixtures to create a wall. Thus, the cordwood is an infill for the walls in a timber frame building, typically between posts. Cordwood masonry can be used in appealing combinations with other techniques (such as rammed earth, cob, or light clay). Construction with cordwood masonry offers a comparatively large thermal mass, which reduces temperature variations.

## EARTHBAG

The most frequent fill material utilized in bag-wall building methods is earth. For footings, foundations, walls, and even vaulted or domed roofs, this construction technique uses stacked polypropylene or natural-fiber (burlap) bags filled with earth or other mixtures devoid of a stabilizer than clay. One of the more often used natural building methods in recent years is construction using earthbags. Rammed-earth constructions that are independent and frequently free-form are made possible. Its rising popularity is because it uses an abundant and frequently on-site available resource (earth) in a potentially affordable building approach that is adaptable, simple to learn, and easy to apply. But because earth is a poor insulator, various filler options are now being investigated in more harsh conditions, replacing all or some of the soil with pumice, rice hulls, or another material with superior insulating value.

## HEMPCRETE

Hempcrete or Hemplime is a bio-composite material used for building and insulation that is made of hemp hurds (shives) and lime (potentially containing natural hydraulic lime, sand, and pozzolans). It is advertised as Hempcrete, Canobiote, Canosmose, and Isochanvre, among other names. Hempcrete is an insulator and moisture controller and is simpler to deal with than conventional lime mixtures. It does not require expansion joints because it is not as brittle as concrete. As a result of combining insulation and thermal mass, the material is lightweight and suitable for most climates.

Hemp grows by absorbing $CO_2$ from the air, storing the carbon, and releasing it as oxygen. This process is similar to that of other plant products. Theoretically, during production, 1 m3 of hempcrete wall may absorb and lock up 165 kg of carbon. In addition, as lime converts into limestone during curing, the carbonation of the lime increases this impact.

A residential grade of concrete has a compressive strength of about 1 MPa or about 1/20 of that. Its low density and resistance to cracking under movement make it an excellent material for usage in earthquake-prone regions. Since hempcrete has a density of 15% lower than conventional concrete, hempcrete walls must be used in conjunction with a frame made of another material to sustain the vertical load.

## RAMMED EARTH

A wall system consisting of compacted earth or another material is known as rammed earth. It is incredibly robust and long-lasting. Quality rammed earth walls have superior low maintenance qualities and are dense, substantial, and stone-like, with great environmental benefits. Rigid insulation can be installed inside the wall as an alternative, depending on the climate. Similarly, based on seismic concerns, bamboo or other naturally tensile materials can be utilized to support the wall.

Since over 10,000 years ago, rammed earth has been used to construct structures, from low-rise to high-rise and from simple huts to elaborate palaces.

Rammed earth walls are created manually or mechanically powered tampers, crushing moist subsoil (which may contain sand, clay, and occasionally gravel) into movable, reusable forms. It is ideal for traditional rammed earth to contain 30% clay and 70% aggregate (gravel, sand). To obtain the desired hue, pigmentation can be added to the mixture. The forms are filled with 5 to 10 inches of mixed moist subsoil, which is then packed completely. This process is continued until the desired height is reached. After the forms are taken down, a structural wall with a lifespan of more than a thousand years is left.

## STONE

Stone has been a common building material for a long time and has long been considered durable. The Giza Pyramids, British Burial Chambers, and Maltese Temples were all constructed out of stone over 4,000 years ago and are still standing today. Dry stone, sometimes referred to as dry stacking, is the earliest type of stone architecture. These are independent structures made of unevenly shaped stones deliberately chosen and arranged to fit snugly together without slipping, such as field walls, bridges, and buildings. Typically, structures are wider at the base and narrower as they heighten. They need the craftsman's talent in selecting and arranging the stones; no extra tools are needed.

Dry stone stacking led to the development of traditional stone masonry. Lime mortar is spread between the stone blocks to secure them in place as they are arranged in rows of uniform (coursed) or unequal (un-coursed) height. Because stone is expensive to quarry, cut, and transport and construction requires a lot of effort and expertise, traditional stone masonry is no longer frequently employed.

Stone is a high thermal mass, extremely durable, and low-maintenance building material. It can be used for floors, walls, arches, and roofs and comes in various shapes, sizes, colors, and textures. Stone is easily recycled for other construction projects and mixes very nicely with the surrounding environment.

**BURLAP BALE**

Although straw and grass have been used in construction in a variety of ways since prehistoric times all over the world, their use in machine-manufactured modular bales appears to have begun in the early 20th century in the midwestern United States, particularly in Nebraska's sandhills, where the grass was abundant and other building materials, even high-quality sods, were not. In a typical straw bale building, rows of bales are stacked one on top of the other with a moisture barrier in between (often in running-bond). Bale walls are frequently fastened together with pins made of bamboo or wood (internally or on their faces) or with surface wire meshes and then plastered or stuccoed with lime-based products or earth/clay renders. Buildings made of straw bales can either have a structural frame made of other materials, with the bales placed in between (serving only as insulation and a base for stucco), known as "infill," or the bales may support the roof and openings, known as "load-bearing" or "Nebraska style," or a combination of framing and load-bearing may be used, known as a "hybrid" straw bale.

However, more recently, higher-density "recompressed" bales (also known as "straw blocks") have increased the loads that may be supported. Field bales may support up to 600 pounds per linear foot of the wall, but the high-density bales bear up to 4,000 lb/lin.ft.

**WOOD FRAME**

By the ninth century, the fundamental components of a timber frame structure—joined timbers, clay walls, and thatch roofs—had been established in Europe and Asia. Until the 19th century, northern cultures frequently built their homes this way. Craftsmanship has always been a key value in timber frame construction. The oldest timber frame buildings, including those in Japan and Scandinavia's stave churches, exhibit expert craftsmanship and a thorough understanding of the technical facets of structural design.

A "bend" is frequently used in timber framing. A bend is a type of structural support that consists of two posts, a tie beam, and two rafters. It is similar to a truss. Through joinery, these are joined together to form a framework. Understanding the bent's fundamental structural elements is necessary for practicing the art. This is the cornerstone of timber frame construction, combined with joinery expertise.

A contemporary method of construction, timber framing is ideal for public structures and the construction of large houses. It is possible to swiftly build a high-performance, a sustainable structure using only natural materials when combined with various natural insulations, timber cladding, and modern lime finishes. There are numerous advantages, including improved building performance over time and decreased waste (much can be recycled, composted, or used as fuel). Cob, straw bale, cordwood/masonry, or other natural building methods are widely utilized in conjunction with timber frame structures.

# Chapter 8:
# Permaculture Education and Outreach

# CHAPTER 8:
# PERMACULTURE EDUCATION AND OUTREACH

For persons in rural locations with plenty of room and land to put the knowledge and training to good use, as well as for those interested in sustainable development work or even for those who wish to decrease their ecological effect, Permaculture can be a terrific career choice. Enroll in a workshop to learn the fundamentals of Permaculture and gain access to cutting-edge ideas like creating a tiny solar electric system or a bicycle-powered pump. Training sessions may also cover the introduction to permaculture and methane biodigesters.

Permaculture education and outreach refer to teaching and promoting permaculture principles, including sustainable agriculture, land use design, and community building. Permaculture education can take many forms, including classroom instruction, hands-on workshops, apprenticeships, and online learning. Outreach efforts may include community gardens, farmers' markets, and other events demonstrating permaculture practices and raising awareness about sustainable living. Permaculture education and outreach aim to empower individuals and communities to design and create regenerative systems that support people and the planet.

Permaculture currently has the most to give the world in terms of equipping people with the knowledge and resources they need to make wise decisions, deal with issues, and come up with innovative solutions at home, at work, in business, in their community, and elsewhere. Ecologist Bill Mollison and environmental designer David Holmgren introduced the

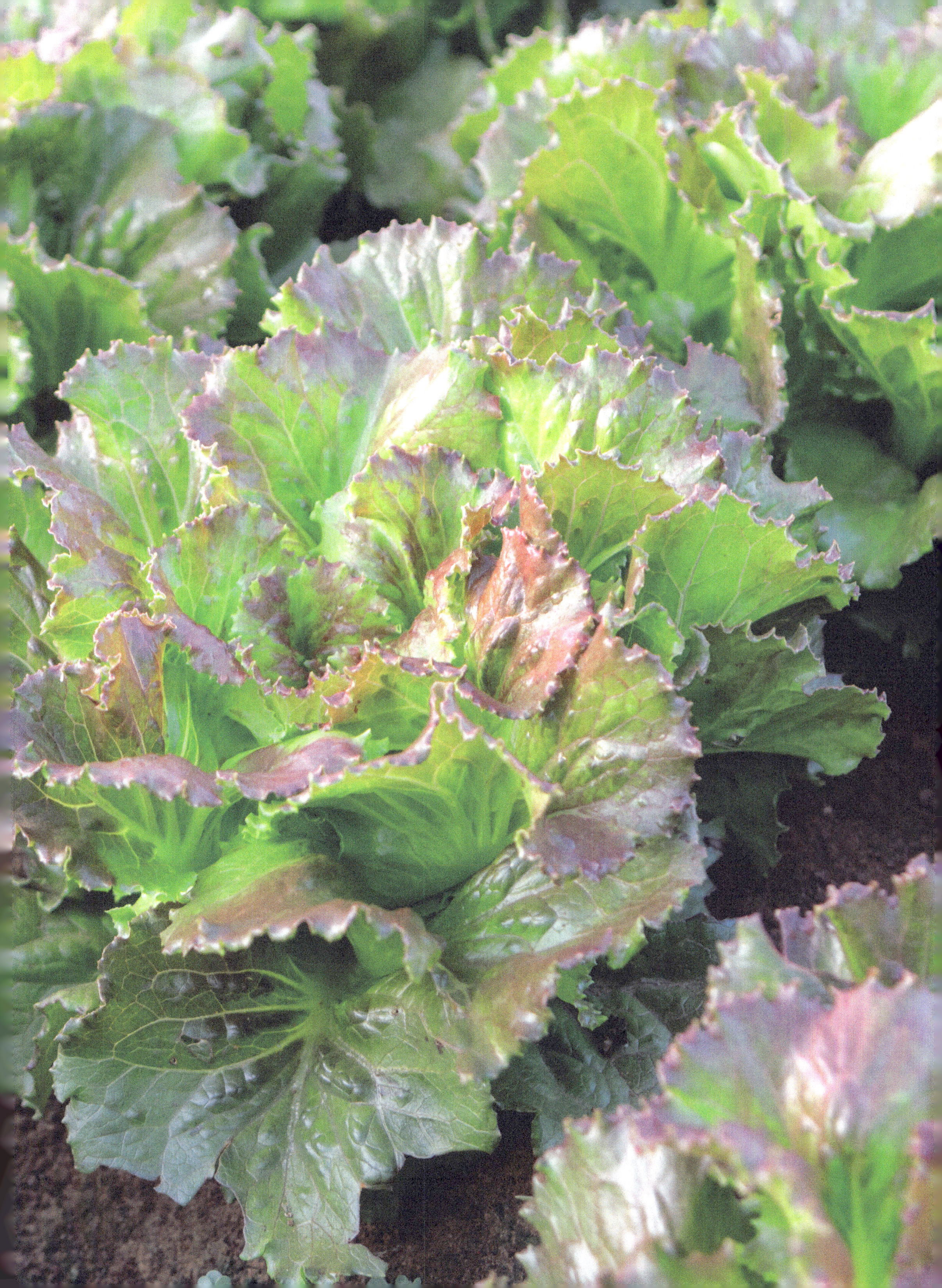

Permaculture concept in Tasmania, Australia, in the middle of the 1970s.

Three decades of international experience at the forefront of sustainable development, design, and living are offered through Permaculture. It integrates a new approach to eco-literacy, environmental science, and social justice as a practical and realistic design system for a sustainable future by drawing on historical lessons and the most sustainable traditional and indigenous wisdom.

The success of Permaculture is based on education-based empowerment. The Permaculture Design Course, or PDC, a rigorous two-week or 72+ hour program, has largely been responsible for this. The basic training needed for permaculture designers and teachers, this course covers every aspect of permaculture design concepts and applications for rural and urban landscapes and lifestyles.

The PDC is said to have been completed by over 500,000 people worldwide, across all countries and climates, who are now enacting significant local, national, and international change. This is a crash course on practical eco-literacy and techniques to lessen your impact, design and create productive settings, create systems for survival, and be a catalyst for change through individual and collective action. It is inspiring and empowering.

## THE COMPLETE GUIDE TO PERMACULTURE COURSES

A balanced system of land repair, known as Permanent Culture, or Permaculture, does not call for any exterior alterations. A very basic permaculture farm feeds its crops with animal feces. When those crops are fed to the animals, a cycle is created. Crops and animal products are coordinated to feed the entire human population. This kind of system develops into a highly complex ecosystem over time.

Studying permaculture courses is the greatest approach to learning about this topic, and seven lessons can be made from them.

## HERE ARE A FEW OF THEIR QUICK DESCRIPTIONS:

The first lesson introduces you to the idea of sustainable living. You'll discover what sustainable living is and what it means to various people.

Lesson 2: The second lesson delves deeply into the idea of permaculture. This lesson gives you a comprehensive overview of the entire procedure, from the system's inception through its operational routines.

Lesson 3: This system's ethics are covered in the third lesson in permaculture courses. In general, there are three different ethics:

caring for the environment, caring for people, and respecting population and consumption limits.

The seventh fundamental of this system is covered in lesson four. The seven guiding principles are diversity, proper scale, reciprocity, stacking function, stacking function repeating, conservation, and giving away surplus.

Lesson 5: You will learn how to put ethics above concepts into practice in this lesson. You learn about the following: a) A three-step approach for developing or redesigning a site; b) Site characteristics; c) How to create a sector; d) Zones. g) The idea of yields and needs.

Lesson 6: In this lesson, you'll learn a few practical methods and approaches for developing and putting a website's design into practice. When you construct or implement a site design, you learn to look into nine areas and the specific methods and techniques required in each of the areas.

The final lesson of a course on permaculture in which you learn more about the subject is lesson seven. A collection of permaculture demonstration sites, details on designs, and how to become a certified design apprentice are all included, as well as a list of relevant websites, books, and articles.

## STRATEGIES FOR EDUCATING OTHERS ABOUT PERMACULTURE AND SPREADING ITS PRINCIPLES AND PRACTICES TO A WIDER AUDIENCE.

Since the introduction of nationally approved vocational training in sustainable systems design and community development in 2003, permaculture education in Australia has advanced to the next stage in preparing individuals to shape and create a sustainable future. The Accredited Permaculture Training(TM) (APT) seeks to prepare the next generation of professionals and tradespeople for a post-carbon society as well as earth stewards and caretakers of the planet.

We must actively take advantage of this crisis's opportunities, respond creatively by embracing change, and take personal and collective responsibility for the kind of world we leave for our children and future generations. Our society is in the process of transitioning to a new and uncertain future.

The most crucial investment you can make in your future as an individual, as well as in your career, family, community, and the planet that sustains you, is to acquire the knowledge, skills, and tools necessary to actively contribute to the creation of a future with a future and to act as a change agent and catalyst. Hands-on workshops and classes:

Practical, hands-on learning experiences are a powerful way to educate people about permaculture and its principles. Workshops can cover various topics, from basic permaculture design to specific techniques such as composting, permaculture gardening, and natural building.

**APPRENTICESHIPS AND INTERNSHIPS:** Giving people the opportunity to work alongside experienced permaculture practitioners is a great way to educate them about the practice and provide them with the skills they need to implement permaculture in their own lives.

**COMMUNITY GARDENS AND DEMONSTRATION SITES:** Creating other demonstration sites showcasing permaculture practices is a great way to educate and inspire people. These sites can be used to host workshops and classes, and they can also be used to provide fresh produce to the community.

**ONLINE LEARNING:** With the rise of online learning platforms, it's now possible to reach a global audience with permaculture education. Online courses, webinars, and e-books can provide permaculture education to people who may not have access to in-person instruction.

**NETWORKING AND COLLABORATIONS:** Permaculture networks can help spread the word about permaculture and its principles. By working with other organizations, permaculture practitioners can share resources and knowledge and collaborate on projects and events.

**ADVOCACY AND AWARENESS CAMPAIGNS:** Raising awareness about permaculture and its benefits through advocacy and awareness campaigns can help to educate people about permaculture and encourage them to adopt sustainable practices in their own lives.

# Chapter 9:
# Permaculture for Health and Wellness

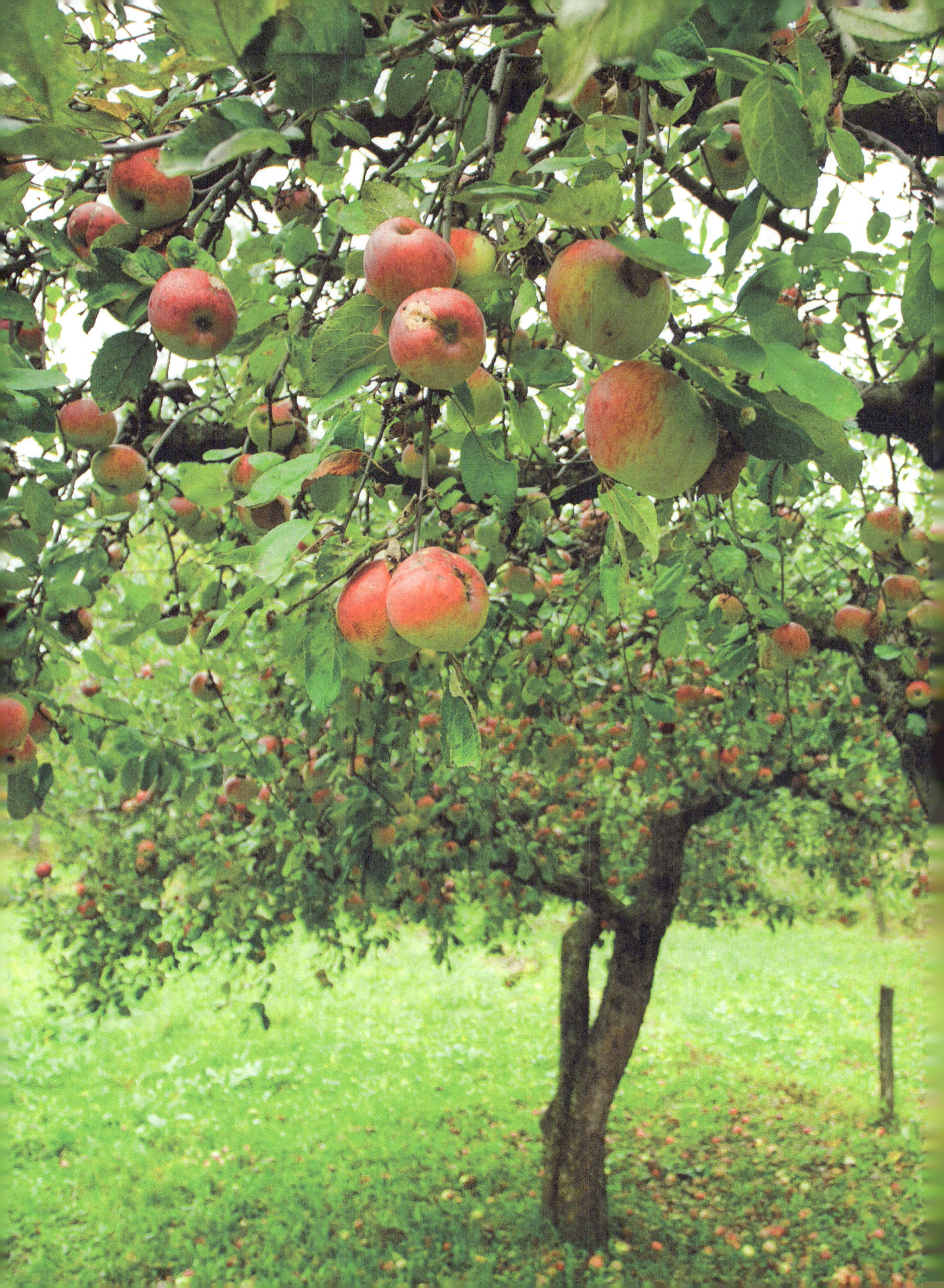

# CHAPTER 9:
# PERMACULTURE FOR HEALTH AND WELLNESS

Our status of being physically and psychologically healthy and disease-free can be used to define health. This brings up the topic of what it takes to develop and maintain a sound body and mind. There is more to this than healthy eating, consistent exercise, and enough sleep. More than just the individual.

The Myth of Separation nature-based contemplation

We are one with nature because it meets our requirements and supplies us with all we need.

Although there is a persistent notion that humans are apart from nature, they are part of nature and subject to its laws. Some individuals are duped into believing that they are somehow above or apart from nature because they believe that the environment is 'out there,' where it may be exploited, harmed, raped, and pillaged without having any negative effects on humankind. Many aspects of how nature functions are more than adequately explained by scientific understanding, but for some people, the science of ecology is an uncomfortable reality.

People often talk of "returning to" or "reconnecting with" nature, yet there is nowhere to go because we can never leave it. The soil is the source of everything we have; it meets our requirements. The bond with nature is also far closer and more personal than people typically realize.

Our bodies are constantly exchanging materials and energy with the environment. Since the beginning of time, nature has recycled and cycled the essential elements that keep us alive: air, water, and food. These elements will continue to do so as they pass through our bodies and return to the intricate natural cycles that sustain all life. Even rusty nails thrown in the ground unintentionally are recycled by nature; their iron may be absorbed by spinach that grows there; when the spinach is consumed, the iron becomes the iron in the hemoglobin in the blood, allowing it to carry oxygen. Even these inanimate items are not apart from ourselves.

Our bodies interchange enormous amounts of material with our environment every second as 10 billion cells die and are replaced by nutrients from the diet. For instance, when we eat plants, they absorb carbon from the air as carbon dioxide gets absorbed into our bodies. Nature and humans are interconnected.

Our bodies are not our own; thus, neither is our health! We beings are part of a web of life and all intricate ecosystems. Ninety percent of the cells in our body are made out of bacteria! These bacteria, found in our mouths, digestive systems, and skin, are crucial to keeping us healthy.

For instance, studies conducted under the direction of Dr. Jeffrey Gordon at the Center for Genome Sciences & Systems Biology at Washington University in St. Louis, USA, have discovered a connection between gut flora and obesity. Lean persons had a wider diversity of gut bacteria species, but obese people had significantly less. Researchers discovered that overweight people have different types and numbers of gut bacteria compared to lean ones. The gut ecology's health was significantly influenced by diet, and, unexpectedly, diets high in processed foods were connected to a less diversified gut ecosystem. An improper diet inhibited the good bacteria from colonizing the gut and increasing, as Gordon's team was able to show in mice.

By this point, it should be evident that internal and external ecosystems affect our health. How can we be healthy if we live in a poisoned, contaminated, and polluted environment? In the end, what we do to nature, we do to ourselves.

Analysis of Human Health Needs from a Permaculture Perspective

The design principle of functional analysis, in which we determine a design element's demands, products, behaviors, and intrinsic qualities, is introduced to us through permaculture. The traditional functional analysis of a chicken is familiar to all permaculture students, but what about a functional analysis of a person? If we conduct a brief, albeit incomplete, functional examination of a human, we can better understand what maintains our physical and mental well-being.

An upright-walking, sociable primate that belongs to the Homo sapiens species that coexists in small groups with other members of its species. Demonstrates a high degree of climate and natural environment adaptation.

Physical needs include access to clean water and air, healthy food, warmth, a place to stay, and protection.

Emotional needs: A sense of community, acceptance, and affection offered by friends, family, and close relationships.

Mental needs: A feeling of self-worth and respect acquired by acknowledgment, focus, competence, mastery, self-confidence, independence, and freedom.

Greater needs: Realizing one's full potential is known as self-actualization. Finding significance and purpose outside oneself, such as via compassion and spirituality, is known as self-transcendence.

We are very sophisticated beings with a variety of demands at various levels. Our physical and emotional health will suffer if these needs are not satisfied.

Our mental state is significant, and mental health is a growing concern, particularly in wealthy first-world nations. By 2020, according to the World Health Organization, mental illness will be the main cause of disease and, as a result, the main cause of income loss in the first world. According to WHO data, unipolar depressive disorders alone were the third most common cause of the global disease burden in 2015 and are expected to top the list by 2030.

Considering the necessity for everyone to at least contemplate becoming more self-sustainable today, given the status of the world economy and climate, I'd say it's even more essential.

To build sustainable ecosystems, Permaculture outlines a universal set of principles that include three main elements that must be taken into account:
- knowledge of how nature functions
- an ethical foundation
- and a design strategy.

This straightforward formula is then used to build a resilient, productive, clean, and healthy community. It might either involve modifying what is currently there or beginning from scratch.

Permaculture is about environmental sustainability and working with the land using principles that minimize any harm to the environment and maximize the output from that terrain and surroundings, as well as sustain human communities by providing them with the necessities to live in harmony with the earth.

Permaculture can have a positive impact on health and wellness in several ways:

**ACCESS TO FRESH, HEALTHY FOOD:** Permaculture gardening and farming techniques can grow a wide variety of fruits and vegetables, giving people access to healthy food. Eating a diet rich in fresh fruits and vegetables can help to prevent chronic diseases and improve overall health.

**INCREASED PHYSICAL ACTIVITY:** Permaculture gardening and farming can be physically demanding, providing an opportunity for people to get regular exercise. This can help to improve cardiovascular health, muscle strength, and overall fitness.

**EXPOSURE TO NATURE:** Permaculture encourages people to spend time in nature, which can positively impact mental and emotional health. Research has shown that spending time in nature can reduce stress, anxiety, and depression.

**BUILDING COMMUNITY:** Permaculture emphasizes the importance of building a community that can benefit mental and emotional health. Social connections and a sense of belonging can help to improve mental well-being and reduce feelings of isolation and loneliness.

**SUSTAINABLE LIVING:** Permaculture encourages sustainable living, which can positively impact the environment and the planet's health. This can promote a sense of purpose and fulfillment and contribute to overall well-being.

It's important to note that a permaculture is a holistic approach that designs, implements, and maintains regenerative, resilient, and sustainable systems. Therefore, it can be used in many applications and sectors, from agriculture to urban design, education to health care, and more.

# Chapter 10:

## • *Permaculture Projects* •

# CHAPTER 10:
## PERMACULTURE PROJECTS

**P**ermaculture projects are designed to create regenerative, resilient, and sustainable systems supporting people and the planet. There are many different types of permaculture projects; some examples include the following:

**FOOD PRODUCTION:** Permaculture gardening and farming projects can grow various fruits and vegetables using crop rotation, companion planting, and natural pest control techniques. These projects can provide fresh, healthy food for the local community and promote food sovereignty.

**WATER MANAGEMENT:** Permaculture projects can be used to manage water resources, such as rainwater harvesting, greywater recycling, and the construction of swales and ponds. These projects can help to conserve water, improve water quality, and reduce the risk of flooding.

**NATURAL BUILDING:** Permaculture projects can be used to design and construct natural buildings, such as straw bale houses, cob houses, and earthbag homes. These buildings are energy-efficient, sustainable, and can be built using locally-sourced materials.

Using natural materials and techniques to construct buildings can reduce the environmental impact of construction and create structures that are in harmony with their surroundings. This can include cob, straw bale, and earthbag building techniques.

*Greenhouse*

*Patio*

*Orchard*

*Grass*

*Trees*

*Stone Sidewalk*

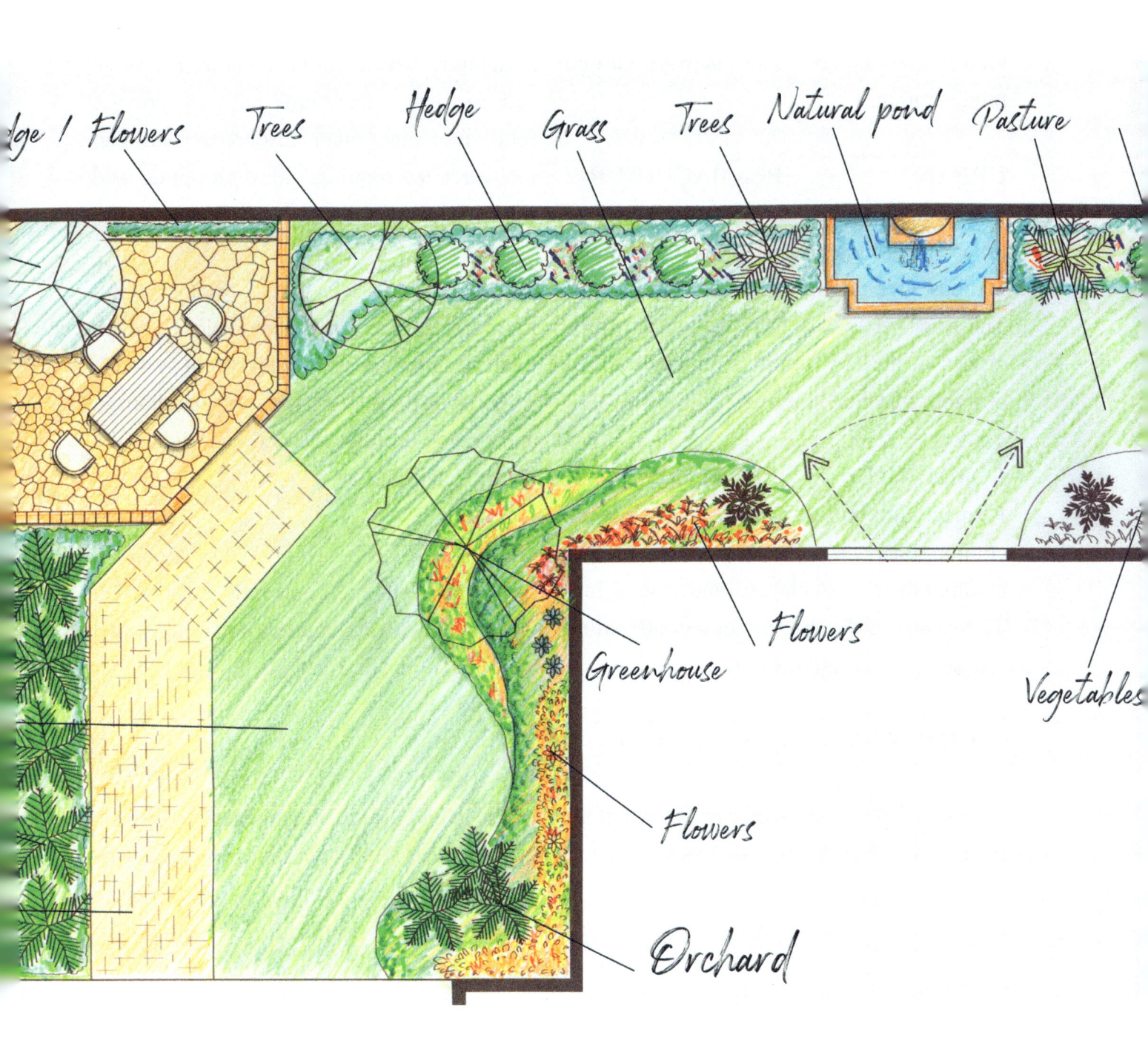

dge / Flowers   Trees   Hedge   Grass   Trees   Natural pond   Pasture

Flowers

Greenhouse

Flowers

Vegetables

Orchard

**LAND RESTORATION:** Permaculture projects can be used to restore degraded land, such as reforestation, soil restoration, and the creation of wildlife habitats. These projects can help improve biodiversity, reduce erosion risk, and increase carbon sequestration.

**URBAN PERMACULTURE:** Permaculture projects can be adapted to urban environments, such as community gardens, green roofs, and urban food forests. These projects can help to create green spaces in the city, improve air quality, and promote sustainable living.

**COMMUNITY DEVELOPMENT:** Permaculture projects can create sustainable communities, such as intentional communities, ecovillages, and cohousing. These projects can promote cooperation, self-sufficiency, and resilience.

**COMMUNITY GARDENS:** Creating a community garden is a great way to unite people and promote permaculture principles of cooperation and self-sufficiency.

Community gardens can include various crops and plants and shared spaces for cooking, eating, and socializing.

**RAINWATER HARVESTING:** Collecting and storing rainwater can help conserve resources and reduce the strain on local water systems. This can be done by installing rain barrels or more complex systems like cisterns or swales.

**AGROFORESTRY:** Agroforestry combines agriculture with forestry, creating a diverse and resilient ecosystem that can provide food, fuel, and other resources. This can include intercropping, alley cropping, and silvopasture.

**PERMACULTURE DESIGN:** Permaculture design is a holistic approach to creating sustainable and resilient systems. This can include designing gardens, homes, and communities harmonious with the natural environment.

**GREEN ROOFS AND WALLS:** Green roofs and walls can help reduce the urban heat island effect, improve air quality and water retention, and provide food and habitat for wildlife.

**COMPOSTING AND VERMICULTURE:** Composting and vermiculture recycle organic waste into nutrient-rich soil. This can help reduce the amount of waste sent to landfills and provide valuable resources for gardening and agriculture.

**FOREST GARDENS:** Forest gardening is a low-maintenance, sustainable way of growing food; it creates a multi-layered food-producing ecosystem, mimicking a woodland ecosystem.

**KEYLINE DESIGN:** Keyline design is a permaculture-based approach to land management that focuses on harnessing the natural flow of water to improve soil fertility, reduce erosion, and increase crop yields.

**ECOVILLAGES:** Ecovillages are intentional communities that apply permaculture principles to create sustainable and resilient living spaces. This can include shared resources, renewable energy systems, and community-based decision-making.

Permaculture projects can be done by individuals, groups, organizations, or governments and can be adapted to different scales, from small-scale home gardens to large-scale projects covering entire regions.

# Chapter 11 :

## • FAQ •

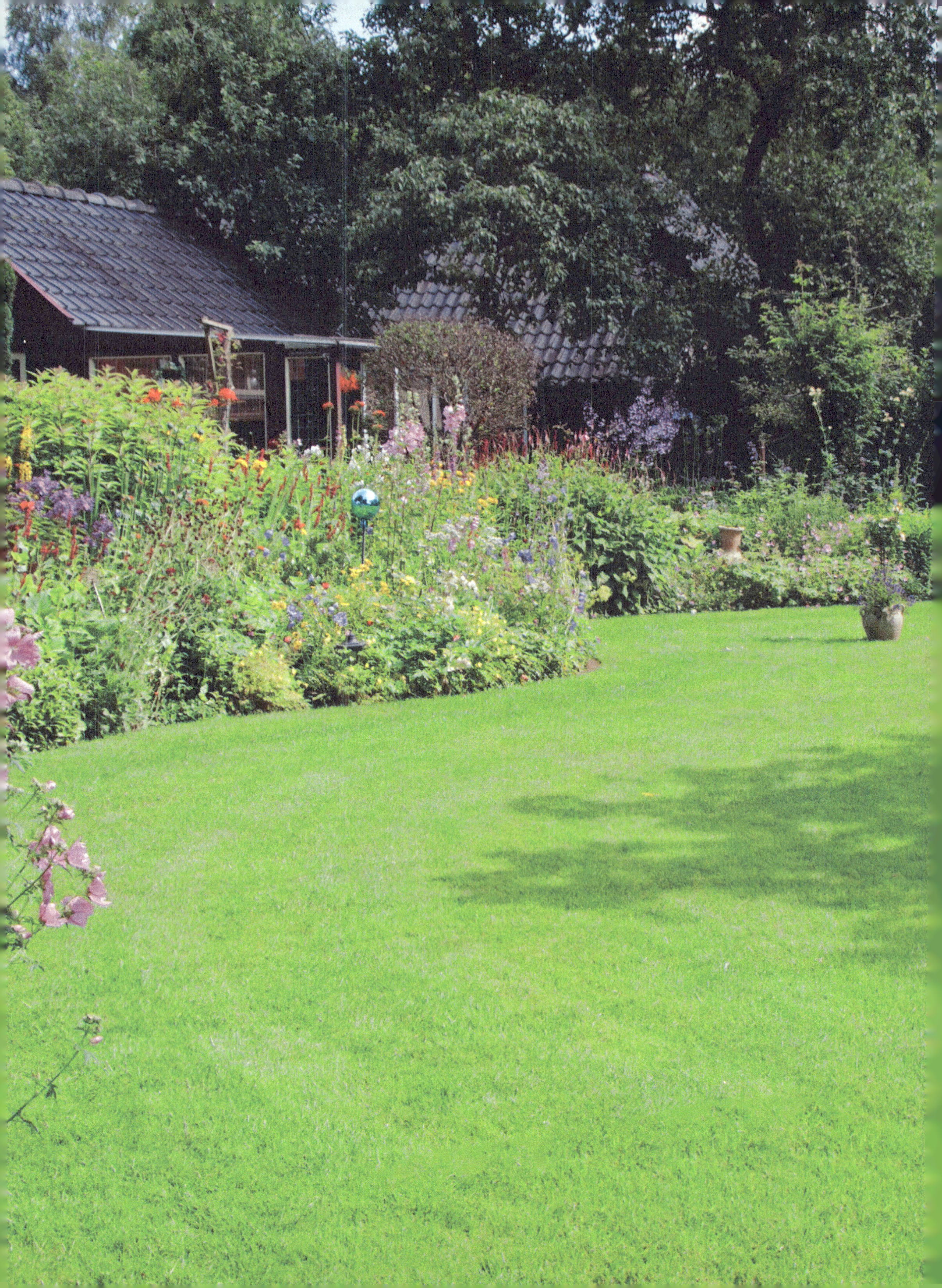

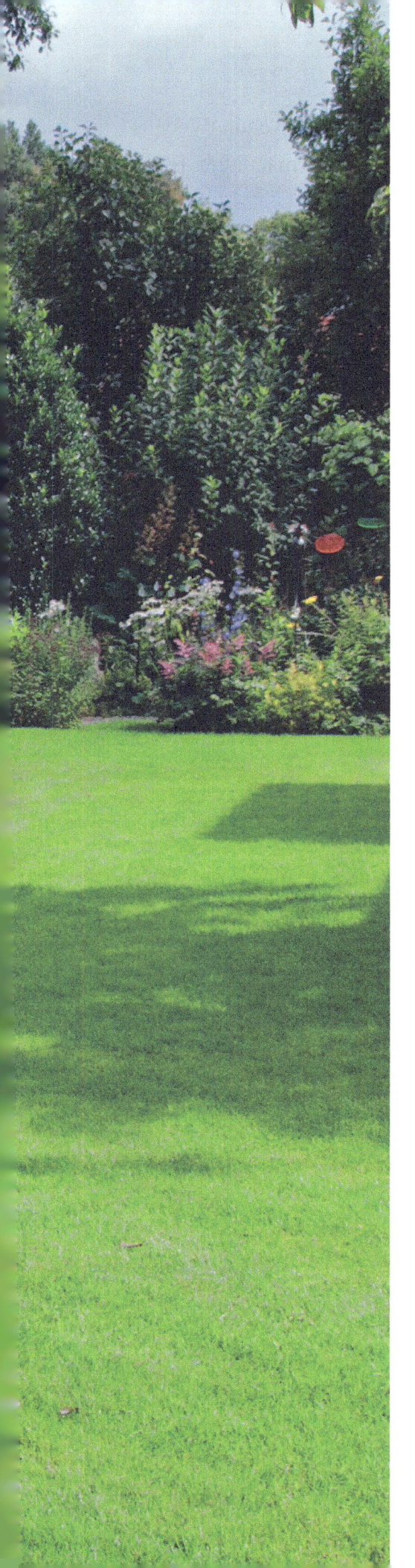

# CHAPTER 11:
# FAQ

**WHAT EXACTLY DOES PERMACULTURE MEAN?**
The word "permaculture" is a combination of the words "permanent" and "agriculture" and refers to the idea of creating a permanent and sustainable form of land use.

As you might have guessed, "permanent culture" is short for "permaculture." The notion is that we will depend increasingly on agriculture that is sustainable and independent of fossil fuels.

It will use regional resources, smaller, more diverse crop planning, and fertilizing without chemicals. The practice of Permaculture promotes a shift away from large, industrial farms and toward more intimate, interdependent farming systems.

**HOW CAN PERMACULTURE BE CREATED AND USED TO OUR ADVANTAGE?**
People can learn how to enhance their home and home farming using permaculture principles from various sources, including books, classes, online tools, and websites. Starting points include planting crops in a specific pattern, rearing livestock in a specific way, or collecting and reusing water for domestic use.

Everyone can profit from Permaculture's evident advantages, and there are many different degrees of permaculture practice.

Additionally, we get to maintain our environment and coexist peacefully with our world and its various ecosystems.

**WHY PERMACULTURE IS GOOD FOR SOCIETY**

Today's society is largely self-centered, and we depend on businesses to provide our demands. We enjoy fast food, disposable items, and affordable fuel, and all of this is unsustainable and will eventually cause a collapse of society. Permaculture is a tool that can help, though.

Permaculture provides a different perspective on the planet and its resources.

# **CONCLUSION**

Permaculture is a concept that produces self-sustaining horticulture and self-sustaining architecture as a subfield of environmental design, ecological design, and ecological engineering. Everything was created using a natural ecology as a model.

The three fundamental tenets of permaculture are respect for the environment, concern for people, and sharing excess. All creatures and humans depend on the planet for survival; therefore, protecting it assures that life will continue and that organisms can reproduce successfully. Mechanisms must be implemented to make resources more accessible because people depend on the earth and the resources it provides. A man may provide for his needs and keep some available resources to take care of the world and those around him, just as natural systems use their outputs to cater to one another.

Two words can nearly perfectly sum up permaculture. First, there is the proverb, "there is a time and a place for everything, and a place for everything in its place," followed by "the whole is more than the sum of its parts." Every natural ingredient must be placed carefully in permaculture to maximize its yield. All components must work together or be connected to create a grand design for this to happen effectively. True, each ingredient is crucial, but the interdependence of the several components is far more crucial.

As a result, permaculture designs are increasingly helpful in regions with small populations but high food needs. It reduces the number of human resources needed and minimizes resource waste. Permaculture employs the notion of zones and sectors to understand how much land is required to feed a certain number of people. The available space is divided into zones, with zone five possibly being the least accessed or used. If zone one's 1000 square meters were permaculture, a family of four could eat nicely.

# REFERENCES

*Permaculture - OpenCommons*. (n.d.). Permaculture - OpenCommons. Retrieved January 28, 2023, from https://opencommons.org/Permaculture

*Permaculture Principle #5: Use and value renewable resources and services | Living Permaculture*. (2020, February 25). Living Permaculture. Retrieved January 28, 2023, from https://livingpermaculturepnw.com/use-and-value-renewable-resources-and-services/

R. (2017, November 8). *Permaculture Design as a Pedagogical Resource*. Resilience. Retrieved January 28, 2023, from https://www.resilience.org/stories/2017-11-08/permaculture-design-as-a-pedagogical-resource/

*What is Permaculture? 5 Ways to Start your Permaculture Garden Today - Permaculture Gardens*. (2021, October 5). Permaculture Gardens. Retrieved January 28, 2023, from https://growmyownfood.com/what-is-permaculture/

A. (2023, January 26). *Organic Farming Methods - Organics Central*. Organics Central. Retrieved January 28, 2023, from https://organicscentral.com/organic-farming-methods/

S. (2007, September 21). *Passive Solar Design - Sustainable Build*. Sustainable Build. Retrieved January 28, 2023, from https://sustainablebuild.co.uk/passivedesign/

*Natural building - Wikipedia*. (2012, June 1). Natural Building - Wikipedia. Retrieved January 28, 2023, from https://en.wikipedia.org/wiki/Natural_building

posts by Angelo (admin), V. A. (2017, January 26). *Permaculture and Health*. Deep Green Permaculture. Retrieved January 28, 2023, from https://deepgreenpermaculture.com/2017/01/26/permaculture-and-health/

*Permaculture: Definition, Principles and Examples*. (2022, September 29). Permaculture: Definition, Principles and Examples. Retrieved January 28, 2023, from https://greenly.earth/en-us/blog/ecology-news/permaculture-definition-principles-and-examples

*Permaculture principles – Brighton Permaculture Trust.* (n.d.). Permaculture Principles – Brighton Permaculture Trust. Retrieved January 28, 2023, from https://brightonpermaculture.org.uk/permaculture/permaculture-principles/

Made in the USA
Coppell, TX
26 February 2023